THE LANGUAGE GYM
SPEAKING BOOKLET III

# SPANISH
## SENTENCE BUILDERS

# TRILOGY
## PART III

A lexicogrammar approach

# SPEAKING BOOKLET

# About the authors

**Gianfranco Conti** taught for 25 years at schools in Italy, the UK and in Kuala Lumpur, Malaysia. He has also been a university lecturer, holds a Master's degree in Applied Linguistics and a PhD in metacognitive strategies as applied to second language writing. He is now an author, a popular independent educational consultant and professional development provider. He has written around 2,000 resources for the TES website, which have awarded him the Best Resources Contributor in 2015. He has co-authored the best-selling and influential book for world languages teachers, "The Language Teacher Toolkit" and "Breaking the sound barrier: Teaching learners how to listen", in which he puts forth his Listening As Modelling methodology. Gianfranco writes an influential blog on second language acquisition called The Language Gym, co-founded the interactive website language-gym.com and the Facebook professional group Global Innovative Language Teachers (GILT). Last but not least, Gianfranco has created the instructional approach known as E.P.I. (Extensive Processing Instruction).

**Dylan Viñales** has taught for 15 years, in schools in Bath, Beijing and Kuala Lumpur in state, independent and international settings. He lives in Kuala Lumpur. He is fluent in five languages, and gets by in several more. Dylan is, besides a teacher, a professional development provider, specialising in E.P.I., metacognition, teaching languages through music (especially ukulele) and cognitive science. In the last five years, together with Dr Conti, he has driven the implementation of E.P.I. in one of the top international schools in the world: Garden International School. This has allowed him to test, on a daily basis, the sequences and activities included in this book with excellent results (his students have won language competitions both locally and internationally). He has designed an original Spanish curriculum, bespoke instructional materials, based on Reading and Listening as Modelling (RAM and LAM). Dylan co-founded the fastest growing professional development group for modern languages teachers on Facebook, Global Innovative Languages Teachers, which includes over 12,000 teachers from all corners of the globe. He authors an influential blog on modern language pedagogy in which he supports the teaching of languages through E.P.I. Dylan is the lead author of Spanish content on the Language Gym website and oversees the technological development of the site.

**Ben Levi** is an innovative language specialist and has been working in the sector since 2018. With a background as a former professional tennis player, Ben's multicultural experiences, particularly in Spain during his formative years and extensive travel while competing globally, ignited his passion for languages. He achieved a 1st Class (Hons) degree in Language Studies and continues to research to develop his knowledge in the field of language learning. Fluent in Spanish and French (as well as English!), with proficiency in other languages, he employs a multifaceted approach to language education, integrating cultural immersion with the E.P.I. teaching methodology. Ben spearheaded the implementation of E.P.I. at his current school and supported curriculum planning in other secondary schools. He has also provided CPD on the effective implementation of E.P.I. to fellow professionals as well as how it can be adapted to other subjects. Active on social media platforms, Ben advocates for language enthusiasts and professionals through his channels, notably Ben Levi Languages on Facebook, Instagram and Twitter, where he shares valuable insights and resources. On TikTok, his educational videos have engaged a wide audience, fostering language appreciation. Continuously innovating, Ben designs novel tasks and language games to inspire learners, nurturing their language proficiency and cultivating a passion for languages.

# Acknowledgements

We would like to thank our editors, Paloma Lozano García, Jaume Llorens and Ryan Cockrell, for their tireless work, proofreading, editing and advising on this book. They are talented, accomplished professionals who work at the highest possible level and add value at every stage of the process. Not only this, but they are also lovely, good-humoured colleagues who go above and beyond, and make the hours of collaborating a real pleasure.

Thanks to Flaticon.com for providing access to a limitless library of engaging icons, clipart and images, which we have used to make this book more user-friendly and engaging for students.

As always, a huge shoutout to our team of incredible educators who helped in checking, and re-checking all the units of this volume: **Hannah Foote, Barry Agnew, Jérôme Nogues, Victoria Harrison, Catalina Petre, María Cristina Caroprese, Ester Borin, Simona Gravina, Sonja Fedrizzi & Ana Amores Márquez** It is thanks to your time, patience, professionalism and detailed feedback that we have been able to produce such a refined and highly accurate product. Your team spirit and good-humour throughout the process also make it a real pleasure to work together.

Finally, our gratitude to the MFL Twitterati for their ongoing support of E.P.I. and the Sentence Builders book series.

**Gracias a todos,**
Gianfranco, Dylan & Ben

# Dedication

### For Catrina
-Gianfranco

### For Ariella & Leonard
-Dylan

### For Olivia & Elsie
-Ben

# Introduction

Hello and welcome to our second Speaking Skills book, designed to be an accompaniment to our Spanish, Extensive Processing Instruction course.

## How to use this book

This book has been designed as a resource to use in conjunction with the E.P.I. approach and teaching strategies in a bid to scaffold oral communication by gradually moving from highly structured tasks (e.g. 'Oral Ping-Pong', 'No Snakes No Ladders', 'Communicative drills') to semi-structured ones (e.g. 'Surveys', 'Things in Common', 'Detectives and Informants').

The activities in this book should be carried out after an intensive listening and reading phase, in which the students have been flooded with highly comprehensible input containing the target vocabulary and grammar structures, thereby processing them receptively many times over.

If following the MARS EARS framework, teachers may want to stage two or three 'chunking-aloud' games, such as 'Mind reading', 'Sentence stealer', 'Lie detector', etc. in order to warm the students up, consolidate good pronunciation and refine their decoding skills.

Also, prior to playing oral retrieval practice games such as 'Oral Ping-Pong', it is recommended that the students do some retrieval practice in writing. This can be done through digital tools, worksheets, mini whiteboards and may be teacher and/or student led.

Finally, it is recommended that, before carrying out the fluency-building games 'Faster', 'Fast and Furious', 'Fluency cards' and Trapdoor', the students be given a few minutes to plan the tasks individually or with peers in order to decrease the potential for cognitive overload and subsequent errors that speaking at increasing speed rate may elicit due to the challenging nature of the task.

## What's inside

The book contains 14 macro-units which concern themselves with a specific communicative function, such as 'Saying what you and others do in your free time', 'Describing our daily routine in the past tense', 'Talking about a recent cinema trip', or 'Talking about our dreams and aspirations'.

Each unit includes a sentence builder with the target constructions and vocabulary followed by a series of tried and tested Conti E.P.I. speaking games, sequenced so as to pose a gradually increasing degree of challenge.

The speaking games included are:

| | |
|---|---|
| o   Oral Ping-Pong | o   Communicative Drills |
| o   Find Someone Who | o   Fluency Cards |
| o   No Snakes No Ladders | o   Trapdoor |
| o   Staircase Translation | o   Things in Common |
| o   Faster! | o   Detectives & Informants |
| o   Fast & Furious | o   Information Gap Tasks |

As already noted, the above games are sequenced in ascending order of linguistic and cognitive challenge. The focus is on gradually building up students' fluency and autonomous competence. These games fall in the 'Structured Production', 'Routinization' and 'Spontaneity' phases in Dr Conti's **MARS EARS** pedagogical cycle, which is central to his E.P.I. approach.

Many thanks for reading this. We hope that both you and your students will find this book useful and enjoyable.

Gianfranco, Dylan & Ben

# SENTENCE BUILDERS TRILOGY - PART III

# SPEAKING BOOKLET

## TABLE OF CONTENTS

# How to play the games – INSTRUCTIONS

**ORAL PING-PONG**

Students work with a partner.

1. Student A starts by reading out his/her first sentence **in English**. Student B must translate **into Spanish**.

2. Student A checks the answer on their sheet. If correct, Student B gets 3 points (100% accurate), 2 points (1 error), or 1 point (correct verb).

3. Student B then reads out his/her first sentence **in English**, Student A translates, and B checks and so on. It is called 'Oral ping-pong translation' because students are firing phrases at each other to translate and score points. **The person with the most points after 10 minutes wins.**

**NOTE:** As a follow-up, students should **write** the translations in the gaps provided.

**FIND SOMEONE WHO**

1. Students are each given a card and a grid to fill in (both provided in each unit of this book).

2. Students must take turns asking the key questions (also provided) and then listening to the information provided by fellow students on their cards.

3. If a student finds someone who matches the criteria in the grid, they write down the person's name.

**TIP:** you will need to set high expectations and then monitor students to make sure they engage in target language and use their speaking & listening skills. Some students may try and bend the rules by copying from friends.

**NO SNAKES NO LADDERS**

Students work in triads. You will need one dice per table and a copy of both the English & Spanish board.

1. One student is the referee and two students are the players.

2. The referee has access to the translations (via a copy of either the English or the Spanish board).

3. Students role a dice and then move their counter forward. They must then translate the language in the box where their counter falls.

4. If a student translates correctly (as confirmed by the referee), they can roll again.

5. If a student cannot translate the content of a square, the referee must tell them the answer, and it is then the other player's turn.

6. When a student wins the game, the referee changes, in order to allow students to alternate roles.

**TIP:** We recommend starting from **Target Language to English**, and then, after a couple of rounds (or whenever students are ready), working from English to Target Language.

**STAIRCASE TRANSLATION**

Students work with a partner.

1. Students must **translate aloud** the paragraph as quickly as possible.

2. Once the whole paragraph has been successfully translated aloud, students write down the translation into the box.

**FASTER**

Students alternate the role of player and referee.

1. Students translate aloud a number of sentences in front of a referee.

2. The student referee provides a time score and some feedback on accuracy.

3. The student listens to feedback and then repeats the process with a second, third, fourth referee with an aim of improving in terms of speed and accuracy on each attempt.

 **TIP:** Make sure that referees have a visible timer to increase motivation!

**FAST & FURIOUS**

Similar to FASTER, but students work from gapped target language sentences.

## COMMUNICATIVE DRILLS

Students alternate the role of player and referee.

1. Students work with a partner to translate short dialogues from English to Spanish.

2. The student referee monitors the game and provides help and feedback on accuracy.

3. Once the students have correctly translated all the boxes out loud, the game is over.

**TIPS:**

- We recommend a rule that whenever the game ends, the referee then faces the winner, or the loser.

- This game can be played with both players working together to translate the squares (collaborating and helping each other), or as a timed challenge (if students are more confident) to translate all 6/9 squares individually with the fastest time.

## FLUENCY CARDS

Students alternate the role of player and referee.

Played like FASTER, students create sentences in the Target Language to match the content of the stimulus grid. There is a mixture of text and images in order to create varied & multi-modal connections to the lexical items and structures being studied.

## THINGS IN COMMON

This activity works like the final SURVEY activity, but focuses on asking closed questions, such as "do you prefer *football* or *basketball?"*

1. Students are given some time to think about their own answers to the questions.

2. Students then ask their peers the questions and make a note of any students that have matching answers (hence 'things in common').

**TIPS:** Students can be given a set time to speak to as many of their peers as possible, or a race to find a certain number of people with a certain number of things in common.

## TRAPDOOR

Students alternate the role of player and referee. Played like FASTER, students translate a set of sentences using the information in the table, which is chunked into several columns as a support.

## DETECTIVES & INFORMANTS

This is a collaborative class game along the lines of **Find Someone Who**.

1. Divide the class into halves.

2. One half - **the detectives**: they have a grid with missing information that they need to fill in. There is one grid per team. This grid must stay at a central location, such as a team home base.

3. One half – **the informants**: they have the answers to the questions.

4. The detectives must ask questions to the informants and then return to their home base to help their team fill in the grid.

## INFORMATION GAP TASK

Without viewing the other person's table, two students need to complete their own table by asking each other questions in Spanish in order to fill in the gaps.

1. Students take turns to ask each other questions and fill in the answers.

2. The game ends when both tables are fully filled in.

## SURVEY

Students ask each other the key questions that have been practised throughout the unit. They then note down key information, either in English or in Spanish on their grid. As a follow-up you could ask students to  write a summary of a friend's information, either in first or third person.

# UNIT 1
## Talking about a past holiday – where we went & where we stayed

| ¿Adónde fuiste de vacaciones? | Where did you go on holiday? |
|---|---|
| ¿Cómo viajaste? | How did you travel? |
| ¿Cómo fue el viaje? | How was the trip? |
| ¿Dónde te quedaste? ¿Te gustó? | Where did you stay? Did you like it? |

| **Fui de vacaciones** | **el verano pasado** | *last summer* | **con mi familia** |
|---|---|---|---|
| *I went on holiday* | **hace un mes / una semana** | *a month ago / a week ago* | *with my family* |

| **Fui a** **Fuimos a** | **Alemania** *Germany* | **los Estados Unidos** *USA* | **Irlanda** *Ireland* |
|---|---|---|---|
| | **China** *China* | **España** *Spain* | **Italia** *Italy* |
| | **Escocia** *Scotland* | **Francia** *France* | **Japón** *Japan* |

| **Viajé** *I travelled* | **en** | **autocar** *coach* | **barco** *boat* | **tren** *train* |
|---|---|---|---|---|
| **Viajamos** *We travelled* | *by* | **avión** *plane* | **coche** *car* | |

| **y el viaje** | **duró** | **una hora.** | **Fue cómodo** *It was comfy* | **Fue largo** *It was long* |
|---|---|---|---|---|
| *and the journey* | *took/lasted* | **dos horas.** | **Fue divertido** *It was fun* | **Fue rápido** *It was quick* |

| ***Me alojé en** *I stayed in* | **un albergue juvenil** *a youth hostel* | **una granja** *a farm* |
|---|---|---|
| **Nos alojamos en** *We stayed in* | **un piso** *a flat* | **un hostal** *a hostel* |
| | **un camping** *a campsite* | **un hotel barato** *a cheap hotel* |
| | | **un hotel de lujo** *a luxury hotel* |
| **Me quedé en** *I stayed in* | **casa de mis abuelos** *my grandparents' house* | |
| **Nos quedamos en** *We stayed in* | | |

| **Me gustó porque** *I liked it because* | **el hotel era genial** *the hotel was great* | **había mucho que hacer** *there was a lot to do* |
|---|---|---|
| **Lo pasé bomba porque** *I had a great time because* | **la gente era simpática** *the people were nice* | **había playas magníficas** *there were superb beaches* |

| **En el hotel** **había** *there was/were* | **un gimnasio** *a gym* | **una cancha de tenis** *a tennis court* |
|---|---|---|
| | **un parque acuático** *a water park* | **una sala de juegos para niños** *a playroom for kids* |
| | **un restaurante** *a restaurant* | **una zona de spa para los padres** *a spa area for parents* |

# UNIT 1 – FIND SOMEONE WHO – Student Cards

| | | | |
|---|---|---|---|
| Fui de vacaciones a Alemania el verano pasado con mi familia.<br><br>**RAQUEL** | Fui a Japón hace un mes y el viaje fue divertido.<br><br>**VERÓNICA** | Nos quedamos en un camping en Francia hace un mes.<br><br>**ROSITA** | Fuimos a Irlanda en avión y el viaje duró una hora.<br><br>**DANIELA** |
| Fuimos a Italia hace una semana.<br><br>**JULIO** | Me quedé en casa de mis abuelos en Escocia.<br><br>**LARA** | Fui a Alemania con mi familia y el viaje fue largo.<br><br>**MARÍA** | Me alojé en un hotel barato en Alemania hace una semana.<br><br>**CARLOS** |
| Viajé en avión y el viaje duró dos horas.<br><br>**MIRABEL** | Fuimos a los Estados Unidos el verano pasado.<br><br>**OLIVIA** | Viajé en coche a Irlanda y el viaje fue cómodo.<br><br>**PACO** | Viajé en barco a Japón y el viaje fue largo.<br><br>**ANDRÉS** |
| Nos alojamos en un hotel de lujo.<br><br>**ÁNGEL** | Viajamos en tren y el viaje fue rápido.<br><br>**PALOMA** | Nos alojamos en un camping en China y el viaje fue divertido.<br><br>**ELSIE** | Nos quedamos en un albergue juvenil el verano pasado.<br><br>**CESC** |

# UNIT 1 – FIND SOMEONE WHO – Student Grid

| ¿Adónde fuiste de vacaciones? | *Where did you go on holiday?* |
|---|---|
| ¿Cómo viajaste? | *How did you travel?* |
| ¿Cómo fue el viaje? | *How was the trip?* |
| ¿Dónde te quedaste? ¿Te gustó? | *Where did you stay? Did you like it?* |

| | Find someone who... | Name(s) |
|---|---|---|
| 1. | ...went to Japan a month ago and the trip was fun. | |
| 2. | ...stayed on a campsite. | |
| 3. | ...went to Ireland by plane and the journey took one hour. | |
| 4. | ...went to Italy a week ago. | |
| 5. | ...stayed at their grandparents' house in Scotland. | |
| 6. | ...went to Germany with their family. | |
| 7. | ...stayed in a cheap hotel or youth hostel. | |
| 8. | ...travelled by plane and the journey took two hours. | |
| 9. | ...went to the USA last summer. | |
| 10. | ...travelled to Ireland by car and the journey was comfy. | |
| 11. | ...travelled to Japan by boat and the journey was long. | |
| 12. | ...stayed in a luxury hotel. | |
| 13. | ...travelled by train. | |

# UNIT 1 – ORAL PING-PONG – Person A

| ENGLISH | SPANISH |
|---|---|
| I went to Scotland. I travelled by coach and the journey took two hours. | Fui a Escocia. Viajé en autocar y el viaje duró dos horas. |
| I stayed in a youth hostel. | |
| The trip took one hour. It was comfy and quick. | El viaje duró una hora. Fue cómodo y rápido. |
| I liked it because the hotel was great. | |
| In the hotel there was a tennis court and a restaurant. | En el hotel había una cancha de tenis y un restaurante. |
| We went to Germany and the trip was long. | |
| I went on holiday last summer with my family. | Fui de vacaciones el verano pasado con mi familia. |
| I stayed at my grandparents' house. I had a great time. | |
| We stayed in a luxury hotel and there was a water park. | Nos alojamos en un hotel de lujo y había un parque acuático. |
| Where did you go on holiday? | |

# UNIT 1 – ORAL PING-PONG – Person B

| ENGLISH | SPANISH |
|---|---|
| I went to Scotland. I travelled by coach and the journey took two hours. | |
| I stayed in a youth hostel. | Me alojé en un albergue juvenil. |
| The trip took one hour. It was comfy and quick. | |
| I liked it because the hotel was great. | Me gustó porque el hotel era genial. |
| In the hotel there was a tennis court and a restaurant. | |
| We went to Germany and the trip was long. | Fuimos a Alemania y el viaje fue largo. |
| I went on holiday last summer with my family. | |
| I stayed at my grandparents' house. I had a great time. | Me quedé en casa de mis abuelos. Lo pasé bomba. |
| We stayed in a luxury hotel and there was a water park. | |
| Where did you go on holiday? | ¿Adónde fuiste de vacaciones? |

# No Snakes No Ladders

| | | | | | |
|---|---|---|---|---|---|
| **START**  | **1** I went to China with my family. | **2** I travelled by plane and the journey took four hours. | **3** I had a great time because the hotel was great. | **4** We stayed in a cheap hotel. | **5** In the hotel there was a gym. |
| | | | | | **6** We travelled by coach and the journey was fun. |
| **15** We stayed in a hostel. | **14** I liked it because there was a lot to do. | **13** We travelled by car and the journey took three hours. | **12** In the hotel there was a playroom for kids. | **11** In the hotel there was a restaurant. | **10** I liked it because the people were friendly. |
| | | | | | **9** We stayed at a campsite and I had a great time. |
| **16** How was the journey? | **17** I went to the USA and the journey was long. | **18** Where did you stay? | **19** I went on holiday to Ireland last summer. | **20** I stayed in a flat and I liked it. | **8** I stayed at my grandparents' house. |
| | | | | **21** In the hotel there was a spa area for parents. | **7** How did you travel? |
| **FINISH** | **30** I liked it because there were superb beaches. | **29** I travelled by boat and the journey was comfy. | **28** In the hotel there was a gym and a tennis court. | **27** I went on holiday a month ago with my family. | **22** We went to Japan and I travelled by plane. |
| | | | | **26** We stayed at my friend's house. | **23** I had a great time because there was a water park. |
| | | | | **25** I travelled by train and the journey took eight hours. | **24** We stayed on a farm. |

# No Snakes No Ladders

| |  |  |  |  |
|---|---|---|---|---|
| | **7** ¿Cómo viajaste? | **8** Me quedé en casa de mis abuelos. | **23** Lo pasé bomba porque había un parque acuático. | **24** Nos alojamos en una granja. |
| | **6** Viajamos en autocar y el viaje fue divertido. | **9** Nos alojamos en un camping y lo pasé bomba. | **22** Fuimos a Japón y viajé en avión. | **25** Viajé en tren y el viaje duró ocho horas. |
| | **5** En el hotel había un gimnasio. | **10** Me gustó porque la gente era simpática. | **21** En el hotel había una zona de spa para los padres. | **26** Nos quedamos en casa de mi amigo/a. |
| | **4** Nos alojamos en un hotel barato. | **11** En el hotel había un restaurante. | **20** Me alojé en un piso y me gustó. | **27** Fui de vacaciones hace un mes con mi familia. |
| | **3** Lo pasé bomba porque el hotel era genial. | **12** En el hotel había una sala de juegos para niños. | **19** Fui de vacaciones a Irlanda el verano pasado. | **28** En el hotel había un gimnasio y una cancha de tenis. |
| | **2** Viajé en avión y el viaje duró cuatro horas. | **13** Viajamos en coche y el viaje duró tres horas. | **18** ¿Dónde te quedaste? | **29** Viajé en barco y el viaje fue cómodo. |
| | **1** Fui a China con mi familia. | **14** Me gustó porque había mucho que hacer. | **17** Fui a los Estados Unidos y el viaje fue largo. | **30** Me gustó porque había playas magníficas. |
| | **SALIDA** | **15** Nos alojamos en un hostal. | **16** ¿Cómo fue el viaje? | **LLEGADA** |

# UNIT 1 – STAIRCASE TRANSLATION

I went on holiday last summer.

I went on holiday last summer with my family. We went to Ireland.

I went on holiday last summer with my family. We went to Ireland. I travelled by boat and the journey took four hours.

I went on holiday last summer with my family. We went to Ireland. I travelled by boat and the journey took four hours. It was long. We stayed in a cheap hotel.

I went on holiday last summer with my family. We went to Ireland. I travelled by boat and the journey took four hours. It was long. We stayed in a cheap hotel. I had a great time because there was a lot to do.

I went on holiday last summer with my family. We went to Ireland. I travelled by boat and the journey took four hours. It was long. We stayed in a cheap hotel. I had a great time because there was a lot to do. In the hotel there was a restaurant and a gym.

**Translate the final step here:**

 # UNIT 1 – FASTER! 

## Say:

1. Where did you go on holiday?

2. I went on holiday a week ago with my family.

3. We went to Scotland.

4. How did you travel?

5. I travelled by plane and car. It was fun.

6. Where did you stay?

7. We stayed in a luxury hotel.

8. Did you like it?

9. I liked it because the people were nice.

10. In the hotel there was a spa area for parents.

|   | Time | Mistakes | Referee's name |
|---|------|----------|----------------|
| 1 |      |          |                |
| 2 |      |          |                |
| 3 |      |          |                |
| 4 |      |          |                |

# UNIT 1 – FAST & FURIOUS – ROUND 1

1. Viajamos en _______________ y el viaje ___________ cinco horas.
   *We travelled by coach and the journey took five hours.*

2. Me ____________ en un albergue _____________ y me gustó.
   *I stayed in a youth hostel and I liked it.*

3. Lo ____________ bomba porque había _____________ magníficas.
   *I had a great time because there were superb beaches.*

4. ¿Dónde te __________________? ¿Te ______________?
   *Where did you stay? Did you like it?*

5. Me quedé en ____________ de mis abuelos y fue _________________.
   *I stayed at my grandparents' house and it was comfortable.*

| | Time 1 | Time 2 | Time 3 | Time 4 |
|---|---|---|---|---|
| **Time** | | | | |
| **Mistakes** | | | | |

# UNIT 1 – FAST & FURIOUS – ROUND 2

1. _________ de vacaciones hace una _________________ con mi familia.
   *I went on holiday a week ago with my family.*

2. Me _____________ porque el hotel ________ genial.
   *I liked it because the hotel was great.*

3. En el hotel ___________ una cancha ____ tenis y una sala de _____________ para niños.
   *In the hotel there was a tennis court and a playroom for kids.*

4. _______________ en tren y el _________ duró ocho horas. ________ largo.
   *We travelled by train and the journey took eight hours. It was long.*

5. ¿ _____________ fuiste de _________________? ¿Cómo fue el __________?
   *Where did you go on holiday? How was the journey?*

| | Time 1 | Time 2 | Time 3 | Time 4 |
|---|---|---|---|---|
| **Time** | | | | |
| **Mistakes** | | | | |

# UNIT 1 – COMMUNICATIVE DRILLS

| 1 | 2 | 3 |
|---|---|---|
| **Where did you go on holiday?**<br><br>- I went on holiday last summer to China. And you?<br><br>**We went to USA.**<br><br>-How fun! | **How did you travel to Spain?**<br><br>- I travelled by coach and the trip took ten hours.<br><br>**How was the trip?**<br><br>- It was very long! | **Last month, I went on holiday to Japan. And you?**<br><br>- Last month, I didn't go on holiday. Last summer, I went on holiday to France. |
| **4** | **5** | **6** |
| **Where did you stay?**<br><br>- I stayed at my grandparents' house.<br><br>**How was the journey?**<br><br>- The journey was fun. We travelled by car and it was comfy. | **I stayed in a youth hostel.**<br><br>- Did you like it?<br><br>**I didn't like it because it wasn't comfy.  And you? Where did you stay?**<br><br>- I stayed in a cheap hotel and it was great. | **Where did you stay?**<br><br>- We stayed on a farm. It was fun.<br><br>**How did you travel?**<br><br>- We travelled by coach and the journey took three hours.<br><br>**Very good.** |
| **7** | **8** | **9** |
| **Where did you go on holiday last summer?**<br><br>- I went on holiday last summer with my family. We went to Italy. And you?<br><br>**We went to Germany a month ago.** | **I went to the United States with my family. Where did you go?**<br><br>- I went to Spain with my friends. It was fun.<br><br>**Very good. I went to Spain last summer.** | **How was the trip?**<br><br>- It was long and fun. We travelled by boat.<br><br>**Very good! Did you like the hotel?**<br><br>- Yes, I had a great time because there was a lot to do. |

| 1 | 2 | 3 |
|---|---|---|
| **¿Adónde fuiste de vacaciones?**<br><br>- Fui de vacaciones el verano pasado a China. ¿Y tú?<br><br>**Fuimos a los Estados Unidos.**<br><br>- ¡Qué divertido! | **¿Cómo viajaste a España?**<br><br>- Viajé en autocar y el viaje duró diez horas.<br><br>**¿Cómo fue el viaje?**<br><br>- ¡Fue muy largo! | **El mes pasado fui de vacaciones a Japón. ¿Y tú?**<br><br>- El mes pasado no fui de vacaciones. El verano pasado fui de vacaciones a Francia. |

| 4 | 5 | 6 |
|---|---|---|
| **¿Dónde te quedaste?**<br><br>- Me quedé en casa de mis abuelos.<br><br>**¿Cómo fue el viaje?**<br><br>- El viaje fue divertido. Viajamos en coche y fue cómodo. | **Me alojé en un albergue juvenil.**<br><br>- ¿Te gustó?<br><br>**No me gustó porque no fue cómodo.  ¿Y tú? ¿Dónde te quedaste?**<br><br>-  Me alojé en un hotel barato y fue genial. | **¿Dónde te quedaste?**<br><br>- Nos alojamos en una granja. Fue divertido.<br><br>**¿Cómo viajaste?**<br><br>- Viajamos en autocar y el viaje duró tres horas.<br><br>**Muy bien.** |

| 7 | 8 | 9 |
|---|---|---|
| **¿Adónde fuiste de vacaciones el verano pasado?**<br><br>- Fui de vacaciones el verano pasado con mi familia. Fuimos a Italia. ¿Y tú?<br><br>**Fuimos a Alemania hace un mes.** | **Fui a los Estados Unidos con mi familia. ¿Adónde fuiste?**<br><br>- Fui a España con mis amigos. Fue divertido.<br><br>**Muy bien. Fui a España el verano pasado.** | **¿Cómo fue el viaje?**<br><br>- Fue largo y divertido. Viajamos en barco.<br><br>**¡Muy bien! ¿Te gustó el hotel?**<br><br>- Sí, lo pasé bomba porque había mucho que hacer. |

# UNIT 1 – SURVEY

| | ¿Cómo te llamas?<br>*What is your name?* | ¿Adónde fuiste de vacaciones?<br>*Where did you go on holiday?* | ¿Cómo viajaste?<br>*How did you travel?* | ¿Dónde te quedaste?<br>*Where did you stay?* |
|---|---|---|---|---|
| *e.g.* | *Me llamo Juan.* | *Fui a Italia.* | *Viajamos en autocar.* | *Me alojé en un hotel barato.* |
| 1. | | | | |
| 2. | | | | |
| 3. | | | | |
| 4. | | | | |
| 5. | | | | |
| 6. | | | | |
| 7. | | | | |
| 8. | | | | |
| 9. | | | | |

# UNIT 1 – ANSWERS

## FIND SOMEONE WHO

| Find someone who... | | Name(s) |
|---|---|---|
| **1.** | ...went to Japan a month ago and the trip was fun. | **Verónica** |
| **2.** | ...stayed on a campsite. | **Rosita/Elsie** |
| **3.** | ...went to Ireland by plane and the trip took one hour. | **Daniela** |
| **4.** | ...went to Italy a week ago. | **Julio** |
| **5.** | ...stayed at their grandparents' house in Scotland. | **Lara** |
| **6.** | ...went to Germany with their family. | **María/Raquel** |
| **7.** | ...stayed in a cheap hotel or youth hostel. | **Carlos/Cesc** |
| **8.** | ...travelled by plane and the trip took two hours. | **Mirabel** |
| **9.** | ...went to the USA last summer. | **Olivia** |
| **10.** | ...travelled to Ireland by car and the trip was comfy. | **Paco** |
| **11.** | ...travelled to Japan by boat and the trip was long. | **Andrés** |
| **12.** | ...stayed in a luxury hotel. | **Ángel** |
| **13.** | ...travelled by train. | **Paloma** |

## STAIRCASE TRANSLATION

Fui de vacaciones el verano pasado con mi familia. Fuimos a Irlanda. Viajé en barco y el viaje duró cuatro horas. Fue largo. Nos alojamos en un hotel barato. Lo pasé bomba porque había mucho que hacer. En el hotel había un restaurante y un gimnasio.

## FASTER!

### REFEREE SOLUTION

1. ¿Adónde fuiste de vacaciones?
2. Fui de vacaciones hace una semana con mi familia.
3. Fuimos a Escocia.
4. ¿Cómo viajaste?
5. Viajé en avión y coche. Fue divertido.
6. ¿Dónde te quedaste?
7. Nos alojamos en un hotel de lujo.
8. ¿Te gustó?
9. Me gustó porque la gente era simpática.
10. En el hotel había una zona de spa para los padres.

## FAST & FURIOUS

### ROUND 1

1. Viajamos en **autocar** y el viaje **duró** cinco horas.
2. Me **alojé** en un albergue **juvenil** y me gustó.
3. Lo **pasé** bomba porque había **playas** magníficas.
4. ¿Dónde te **quedaste**? ¿Te **gustó**?
5. Me quedé en **casa** de mis abuelos y fue **cómodo**.

### ROUND 2

1. **Fui** de vacaciones hace una **semana** con mi familia.
2. Me **gustó** porque el hotel **era** genial.
3. En el hotel **había** una cancha **de** tenis y una sala de **juegos** para niños.
4. **Viajamos** en tren y el **viaje** duró ocho horas. **Fue** largo.
5. ¿**Adónde** fuiste de **vacaciones**? ¿Cómo fue el **viaje**?

# UNIT 2.

## Talking about a past holiday – what we did and our opinion of it

| ¿Qué hiciste durante las vacaciones? | *What did you do during the holidays?* |
|---|---|
| ¿Qué fue lo mejor de tus vacaciones? | *What was the best thing about your holidays?* |

| Durante las vacaciones *During the holidays* | **hice muchas cosas** | *I did many things* | | |
|---|---|---|---|---|
| | **no hice casi nada** | *I did hardly anything* | | |
| | **pasé tiempo** | *I spent time* | **con mi familia** | *with my family* |
| | | | **solo/a** | *alone* |

| **El primer día** | *On the first day* | **El segundo día** | *On the second day* |
|---|---|---|---|
| **alquilé una bici** | *I rented a bike* | **di un paseo** | *I went for a walk* |
| **comí comida deliciosa** | *I ate delicious food* | **jugué con mi primo** | *I played with my cousin* |
| **compré recuerdos** | *I bought souvenirs* | **nadé en el mar** | *I swam in the sea* |
| **conocí a un chico simpático** | *I met a nice boy* | **probé platos típicos** | *I tried typical dishes* |
| **conocí a una chica simpática** | *I met a nice girl* | **saqué fotos** | *I took photos* |
| **descansé en la playa** | *I rested on the beach* | **tomé el sol** | *I sunbathed* |

| **Muchos días** *On many days* | **me acosté tarde** *I went to bed late* | **me desperté tarde** *I got up late* |
|---|---|---|

| **Por la mañana** *In the morning* **Por la tarde** *In the afternoon* **Por la noche** *At night* | **fui** *I went* **fuimos** *we went* | **al centro de la ciudad** *to the city centre* **al centro comercial** *to the shopping mall* **al parque** *to the park* **a la playa** *to the beach* **a la montaña** *to the mountain* | **para** *to* | **comprar cosas** *buy things* **nadar en el mar** *swim in the sea* **ir de tiendas** *go shopping* **tomar el sol** *sunbathe* **tomar un helado** *have an ice cream* |
|---|---|---|---|---|
| | ***hice** *I did* **hicimos** *we did* | **buceo** *diving* **natación** *swimming* | **senderismo** *hiking* **turismo** *sightseeing* | |

| **Lo mejor fue cuando...** | *The best thing was when...* | | |
|---|---|---|---|
| **...cené en un restaurante** | *I had dinner in a restaurant* | | **mi mejor amigo/a** *my best friend* |
| **...pasé tiempo** | *I spent time* | **con** | **mi familia** *my family* |
| **...vi un partido de fútbol** | *I watched a football match* | | **mis abuelos** *my grandparents* |

| **En mi opinión** *In my opinion* | **fueron unas vacaciones** *they were ... holidays* | **inolvidables** *unforgettable* **buenísimas/malísimas** *really really good/bad* | |
|---|---|---|---|
| **y** *and* **pero** *but* | **(no) me gustaría** *I would -not- like* | **volver** *to go back* | **el próximo año** *next year* |

***Author's note: In Spanish *hacer* means "to do" and is often used in combination with actions and activities. However, watch out, because sentences such as *HICE natación* are translated back into natural English as "I swam" or "I WENT swimming".**

# UNIT 2 – FIND SOMEONE WHO – Student Cards

| | | | |
|---|---|---|---|
| El primer día compré recuerdos.<br><br>**PEPA** | Por la mañana fuimos al parque para tomar un helado.<br><br>**SIMÓN** | El segundo día jugué con mi primo.<br><br>**JILL** | Por la noche fui al centro de la ciudad para ir de tiendas.<br><br>**PASQUAL** |
| Por la tarde conocí a un chico simpático.<br><br>**ALBERTO** | Durante las vacaciones pasé tiempo solo.<br><br>**FRANCISCO** | Muchos días me desperté tarde.<br><br>**WILLIAM** | Por la noche hicimos senderismo.<br><br>**VERÓNICA** |
| El primer día nadé en el mar y comí comida deliciosa.<br><br>**FRAN** | Durante las vacaciones nadé en el mar y alquilé una bici.<br><br>**ENRICO** | Por la mañana fuimos a la montaña. Por la tarde fui al centro comercial.<br><br>**TOMÁS** | Durante las vacaciones no hice casi nada.<br><br>**NORBERTO** |
| El segundo día fui al centro de la ciudad para comprar cosas.<br><br>**RAE** | Muchos días me acosté tarde.<br><br>**LAUTARO** | Por la tarde hice buceo y nadé en el mar.<br><br>**JAIME** | El primer día vi un partido de fútbol.<br><br>**ANTONIO** |

# UNIT 2 – FIND SOMEONE WHO – Student Grid

| **¿Qué hiciste durante las vacaciones?** *What did you do during the holidays?* | |
|---|---|
| **Find someone who...** | **Name(s)** |
| 1. ...went shopping in the city centre at night. | |
| 2. ...woke up or went to bed late many days. | |
| 3. ...met a nice boy in the afternoon. | |
| 4. ...watched a football match on the first day. | |
| 5. ...went to the park to have ice cream in the morning. | |
| 6. ...swam in the sea during the holiday. | |
| 7. ...played with their cousin on the second day. | |
| 8. ...did almost nothing during the holiday or spent time on their own. | |
| 9. ...swam in the sea and ate delicious food on the first day. | |
| 10. ...bought souvenirs on the first day. | |
| 11. ...went to shopping mall in the afternoon. | |
| 12. ...went to the city centre to buy things on the second day. | |
| 13. ...went hiking at night! | |

# UNIT 2 – ORAL PING-PONG – Person A

| ENGLISH | SPANISH |
|---|---|
| The best thing was when I spent time with my grandparents. | Lo mejor fue cuando pasé tiempo con mis abuelos. |
| During the holidays, I spent time alone. | |
| At night, I went to the city centre to buy things. | Por la noche fui al centro de la ciudad para comprar cosas. |
| On many days, I went to bed late. | |
| On the first day, I rested on the beach. | El primer día descansé en la playa. |
| What did you do during the holidays? | |
| In my opinion, they were unforgettable holidays. | En mi opinión fueron unas vacaciones inolvidables. |
| In the morning, I swam in the sea with my family. | |
| What was the best thing about your holidays? | ¿Qué fue lo mejor de tus vacaciones? |
| The best thing was when I had dinner at a restaurant with my best friend. | |

# UNIT 2 – ORAL PING-PONG – Person B

| ENGLISH | SPANISH |
| --- | --- |
| The best thing was when I spent time with my grandparents. | |
| During the holidays, I spent time alone. | Durante las vacaciones pasé tiempo solo/a. |
| At night, I went to the city centre to buy things. | |
| On many days, I went to bed late. | Muchos días me acosté tarde. |
| On the first day, I rested on the beach. | |
| What did you do during the holidays? | ¿Qué hiciste durante las vacaciones? |
| In my opinion, they were unforgettable holidays. | |
| In the morning, I swam in the sea with my family. | Por la mañana nadé en el mar con mi familia. |
| What was the best thing about your holidays? | |
| The best thing was when I had dinner at a restaurant with my best friend. | Lo mejor fue cuando cené en un restaurante con mi mejor amigo/a. |

# No Snakes No Ladders

**START**

**1** — During the holidays, I spent time with my family.

**2** — On the second day, I bought souvenirs.

**3** — On many days, I went to bed late.

**4** — In the afternoon, we did hiking.

**5** — The best thing was when I spent time with my family.

**6** — On the first day, I met a nice girl.

**7** — During the holidays, I spent time alone.

**8** — In the afternoon, I went to the beach to have an ice cream.

**9** — The best thing was when I watched a football match.

**10** — In my opinion, they were unforgettable holidays.

**11** — During the holidays, I ate delicious food.

**12** — I would like to go back next year.

**13** — In the afternoon, I did diving.

**14** — At night, we went to the shopping mall.

**15** — We did hiking and diving.

**16** — On the second day, I took photos on the beach.

**17** — On the first day, I did hardly anything.

**18** — At night, I went to the park to have an ice cream.

**19** — The best thing was when I had dinner in a restaurant.

**20** — On the first day, I rested on the beach and I sunbathed.

**21** — On many days, I went to the beach.

**22** — During the holidays, I rented a bike.

**23** — In my opinion, they were really really good holidays.

**24** — I would not like to go back to the mountain.

**25** — On the first day, I played with my cousin.

**26** — In the morning, I swam in the sea and I went for a walk.

**27** — The best thing was when I bought souvenirs.

**28** — They were really really bad holidays and I would not like to go back.

**29** — What was the best thing about your holidays?

**30** — On many days, I got up late.

**FINISH**

# No Snakes No Ladders

**SALIDA**

**1** — Durante las vacaciones pasé tiempo con mi familia.

**2** — El segundo día compré recuerdos.

**3** — Muchos días me acosté tarde.

**4** — Por la tarde hicimos senderismo.

**5** — Lo mejor fue cuando pasé tiempo con mi familia.

**6** — El primer día conocí a una chica simpática.

**7** — Durante las vacaciones pasé tiempo solo/a.

**8** — Por la tarde fui a la playa para tomar un helado.

**9** — Lo mejor fue cuando vi un partido de fútbol.

**10** — En mi opinión fueron unas vacaciones inolvidables.

**11** — Durante las vacaciones comí comida deliciosa.

**12** — Me gustaría volver el próximo año.

**13** — Por la tarde hice buceo.

**14** — Por la noche fuimos al centro comercial.

**15** — Hicimos senderismo y buceo.

**16** — El segundo día saqué fotos en la playa.

**17** — El primer día no hice casi nada.

**18** — Por la noche fui al parque para tomar un helado.

**19** — Lo mejor fue cuando cené en un restaurante.

**20** — El primer día descansé en la playa y tomé el sol.

**21** — Muchos días fui a la playa.

**22** — Durante las vacaciones alquilé una bici.

**23** — En mi opinión fueron unas vacaciones buenísimas.

**24** — No me gustaría volver a la montaña.

**25** — El primer día jugué con mi primo/a.

**26** — Por la mañana nadé en el mar y di un paseo.

**27** — Lo mejor fue cuando compré recuerdos.

**28** — Fueron unas vacaciones malísimas y no me gustaría volver.

**29** — ¿Qué fue lo mejor de tus vacaciones?

**30** — Muchos días me desperté tarde.

**LLEGADA**

# UNIT 2 – STAIRCASE TRANSLATION

During the holidays

During the holidays, I did many things.

During the holidays, I did many things. On the first day, I rested on the beach.

During the holidays, I did many things. On the first day, I rested on the beach. On the second day, I went to the city centre to buy things.

During the holidays, I did many things. On the first day, I rested on the beach. On the second day, I went to the city centre to buy things. In the afternoon, we did sightseeing and I took photos.

During the holidays, I did many things. On the first day, I rested on the beach. On the second day, I went to the city centre to buy things. In the afternoon, we did sightseeing and I took photos. The best thing was when I had dinner in a restuarant with my grandparents.

**Translate the last step here:**

#  UNIT 2 – FASTER! 

**Say:**

1. What did you do during the holidays?

2. During the holidays, I spent time with my family.

3. On the first day, I ate delicious food.

4. On the second day, I met a nice boy.

5. On many days, I went to bed late.

6. What was the best thing about your holidays?

7. The best thing was when I watched a football match with my best friend.

8. In my opinion, they were unforgettable holidays.

9. I would like to go back next year.

10. At night, we went to the city centre to buy things.

|  | Time | Mistakes | Referee's name |
|---|---|---|---|
| 1 |  |  |  |
| 2 |  |  |  |
| 3 |  |  |  |
| 4 |  |  |  |

# UNIT 2 – TRAPDOOR

| El primer día<br>El segundo día<br>Por la mañana<br>Por la tarde<br>Por la noche | fui<br>fuimos | al parque<br>a la playa<br>a la montaña<br>al centro comercial<br>al centro de la ciudad | para | nadar en el mar<br>comprar cosas<br>tomar el sol<br>tomar un helado<br>ir de tiendas |
| --- | --- | --- | --- | --- |
| | hice<br>hicimos | buceo<br>natación<br>senderismo<br>turismo | y | descansé en la playa<br>comí comida deliciosa<br>tomé el sol<br>di un paseo |

## ROUND 1

1. On the first day, I went to the shopping mall to buy things.
2. In the morning, I did diving and I sunbathed.
3. At night, we went to the city centre to go shopping.
4. In the afternoon, we did hiking and I went for a walk.
5. On the second day, I went to the park to have an ice cream.
6. In the morning, I did sightseeing and I ate delicious food.
7. In the afternoon, we went to the beach to swim in the sea.

| | Time 1 | Time 2 | Time 3 | Time 4 |
| --- | --- | --- | --- | --- |
| **Time** | | | | |
| **Mistakes** | | | | |

## ROUND 2

1. On the second day, I went to the beach to have an ice cream.
2. In the afternoon, we did swimming and I sunbathed.
3. On the first day, we went to the city centre and I went for a walk.
4. In the morning, I went to the mountain and in the afternoon, I went to the beach.
5. On the second day, I went to the park to sunbathe.
6. At night, I did sightseeing and I ate delicious food.
7. In the afternoon, we did diving and I rested on the beach.

| | Time 1 | Time 2 | Time 3 | Time 4 |
| --- | --- | --- | --- | --- |
| **Time** | | | | |
| **Mistakes** | | | | |

# UNIT 2 – COMMUNICATIVE DRILLS

| 1 | 2 | 3 |
|---|---|---|
| **Hello! What did you do during the holidays?**<br><br>- During the holidays, I spent time with my family.<br><br>**What did you do on the first day?**<br><br>- On the first day, I rested on the beach and sunbathed. | **Good morning!**<br><br>-Hello! During the holidays, I did hardly anything. And you?<br><br>**In the morning, I went to the park to have an ice cream.**<br><br>- I went to the park too. I played with my cousin. | **Hello! What was the best thing about your holidays?**<br><br>- The best thing was when I watched a football match with my family.<br><br>**Very good. In my opinion, they were really really good holidays.** |
| 4 | 5 | 6 |
| **What did you do in the morning?**<br><br>- In the morning, I went to the city centre to go shopping.<br><br>**What did you do at night?**<br><br>- At night, I went sightseeing and ate delicious food.<br><br>**Good!** | **Hello. How are you?**<br><br>-Very good, thank you. What did you do during the holidays?<br><br>**On the first day, I rented a bike and the second day I bought souvenirs.**<br><br>Interesting. During my holidays, I rested on the beach. | **What did you do in the afternoon on holiday?**<br><br>- In the afternoon, I had dinner in a restaurant with my grandparents and I tried typical dishes.<br><br>**What was the best thing about your holidays?**<br><br>- The best thing was when I met a nice girl. |
| 7 | 8 | 9 |
| **Good afternoon!**<br><br>-Hello! What did you do during the holidays?<br><br>**On many days, I went to bed late and woke up late.**<br><br>-Good. In the afternoon, I rested on the beach. I would like to go back next year. | **How are you?**<br><br>-Very good. And you? What did you do on the first day of your holidays?<br><br>**Good, thank you. On the first day, I bought souvenirs with my best friend. And you?**<br><br>On the first day, I did hardly anything. | **What did you do at night?**<br><br>- At night, I went to bed late. On many days, I swam in the sea.<br><br>**What did you do in the morning?**<br><br>- In the morning, I woke up late and took a walk alone.<br><br>**I spent time alone too.** |

# UNIT 2 – COMMUNICATIVE DRILLS
## REFEREE CARD

| 1 | 2 | 3 |
|---|---|---|
| **¡Hola! ¿Qué hiciste durante las vacaciones?**<br><br>- Durante las vacaciones pasé tiempo con mi familia.<br><br>**¿Qué hiciste el primer día?**<br><br>- El primer día descansé en la playa y tomé el sol. | **¡Buenos días!**<br><br>- ¡Hola! Durante las vacaciones no hice casi nada. ¿Y tú?<br><br>**Por la mañana fui al parque para tomar un helado.**<br><br>- Yo también fui al parque. Jugué con mi primo/a. | **¡Hola! ¿Qué fue lo mejor de tus vacaciones?**<br><br>- Lo mejor fue cuando vi un partido de fútbol con mi familia.<br><br>**Muy bien. En mi opinión fueron unas vacaciones buenísimas.** |
| **4** | **5** | **6** |
| **¿Qué hiciste por la mañana?**<br><br>- Por la mañana fui al centro de la ciudad para ir de tiendas.<br><br>**¿Qué hiciste por la noche?**<br><br>- Por la noche hice turismo y comí comida deliciosa.<br><br>**¡Bien!** | **Hola. ¿Qué tal?**<br><br>- Muy bien gracias. ¿Qué hiciste durante las vacaciones?<br><br>**El primer día alquilé una bici y el segundo día compré recuerdos.**<br><br>Interesante. Durante mis vacaciones descansé en la playa. | **¿Qué hiciste por la tarde en las vacaciones?**<br><br>- Por la tarde cené en un restaurante con mis abuelos y probé platos típicos.<br><br>**¿Qué fue lo mejor de tus vacaciones?**<br><br>- Lo mejor fue cuando conocí a una chica simpática. |
| **7** | **8** | **9** |
| **¡Buenas tardes!**<br><br>- ¡Hola! ¿Qué hiciste durante las vacaciones?<br><br>**Muchos días me acosté tarde y me desperté tarde.**<br><br>- Bien. Por la tarde descansé en la playa. Me gustaría volver el próximo año. | **¿Qué tal?**<br><br>- Muy bien. ¿Y tú? ¿Qué hiciste el primer día de tus vacaciones?<br><br>**Bien, gracias. El primer día compré recuerdos con mi mejor amigo/a. ¿Y tú?**<br><br>El primer día no hice casi nada. | **¿Qué hiciste por la noche?**<br><br>- Por la noche me acosté tarde. Muchos días nadé en el mar.<br><br>**¿Qué hiciste por la mañana?**<br><br>- Por la mañana me desperté tarde y di un paseo solo/a.<br><br>**Pasé tiempo solo/a también.** |

# UNIT 2 – SURVEY

| | ¿Cómo te llamas?<br>*What is your name?* | ¿Qué hiciste durante las vacaciones?<br>*What did you do during the holidays?* | ¿Qué hiciste el primer día?<br>*What did you do on the first day?* | ¿Qué hiciste por la mañana?<br>*What did you do in the morning?* | ¿Qué fue lo mejor de tus vacaciones?<br>*What was the best thing about your holidays?* |
|---|---|---|---|---|---|
| *e.g.* | *Me llamo Juan.* | *Durante las vacaciones pasé tiempo con mi familia.* | *El primer día descansé en la playa.* | *Por la mañana fui a la playa para tomar un helado.* | *Lo mejor fue cuando cené en un restaurante con mis abuelos.* |
| 1. | | | | | |
| 2. | | | | | |
| 3. | | | | | |
| 4. | | | | | |
| 5. | | | | | |
| 6. | | | | | |
| 7. | | | | | |

# UNIT 2 – ANSWERS

## FIND SOMEONE WHO

| Find someone who... | | Name(s) |
|---|---|---|
| 1. | ...went shopping in the city centre at night. | Pascual |
| 2. | ...woke up or went to bed late many days. | William/Lautaro |
| 3. | ...met a nice boy in the afternoon. | Alberto |
| 4. | ...watched a football match on the first day. | Antonio |
| 5. | ...went to the park to have ice cream in the morning. | Simón |
| 6. | ...swam in the sea during the holiday. | Enrico/Jaime |
| 7. | ...played with their cousin on the second day. | Jill |
| 8. | ...did almost nothing during the holiday or spent time on their own. | Norberto/Francisco |
| 9. | ...swam in the sea and ate delicious food on the first day. | Fran |
| 10. | ...bought souvenirs on the first day. | Pepa |
| 11. | ...went to the shopping mall in the afternoon. | Tomás |
| 12. | ...went to the city centre to buy things on the second day. | Rae |
| 13. | ...went hiking at night! | Verónica |

## STAIRCASE TRANSLATION

Durante las vacaciones hice muchas cosas. El primer día descansé en la playa. El segundo día fui al centro de la ciudad para comprar cosas. Por la tarde hicimos turismo y saqué fotos. Lo mejor fue cuando cené en un restaurante con mis abuelos.

## FASTER! REFEREE SOLUTION:

1. ¿Qué hiciste durante las vacaciones?
2. Durante las vacaciones pasé tiempo con mi familia.
3. El primer día comí comida deliciosa.
4. El segundo día conocí a un chico simpático.
5. Muchos días me acosté tarde.
6. ¿Qué fue lo mejor de tus vacaciones?
7. Lo mejor fue cuando vi un partido de fútbol con mi mejor amigo/a.
8. En mi opinión, fueron unas vacaciones inolvidables.
9. Me gustaría volver el próximo año.
10. Por la noche fuimos al centro de la ciudad para comprar cosas.

## TRAPDOOR

### ROUND 1

1. El primer día fui al centro comercial para comprar cosas.
2. Por la mañana hice buceo y tomé el sol.
3. Por la noche fuimos al centro de la ciudad para ir de tiendas.
4. Por la tarde hicimos senderismo y di un paseo.
5. El segundo día fui al parque para tomar un helado.
6. Por la mañana hice turismo y comí comida deliciosa.
7. Por la tarde fuimos a la playa para nadar en el mar.

### ROUND 2

1. El segundo día fui a la playa para tomar un helado.
2. Por la tarde hicimos natación y tomé el sol.
3. El primer día fuimos al centro de la ciudad y di un paseo.
4. Por la mañana fui a la montaña y por la tarde fui a la playa.
5. El segundo día fui al parque para tomar el sol.
6. Por la noche hice turismo y comí comida deliciosa.
7. Por la tarde hicimos buceo y descansé en la playa.

# UNIT 3.
## Describing a typical day in the present, preterite & near future

| ¿Qué haces normalmente en tu tiempo libre? | What do you normally do in your free time? |
| --- | --- |

### PRESENT (INDICATIVE)

| Por lo general | *In general* | **El fin de semana** | *At the weekend* | **Entre semana** | *During the week* |
| --- | --- | --- | --- | --- | --- |

| | | | |
| --- | --- | --- | --- |
| **arreglo mi dormitorio** | *I tidy my bedroom* | **juego a la Play** | *I play on the PlayStation* |
| **ayudo a mis padres** | *I help my parents* | **juego con mi hermano** | *I play with my brother* |
| **como en un restaurante** | *I eat in a restaurant* | **salgo con mi novio** | *I go out with my boyfriend* |
| **hago mis deberes** | *I do my homework* | **salgo con mi novia** | *I go out with my girlfriend* |
| **monto en bici** | *I ride my bike* | **voy al centro comercial** | *I go to the shopping mall* |

| **Me gusta** | *I like (to)* | **Suelo** | *I usually* | **Tengo que** | *I have to* |
| --- | --- | --- | --- | --- | --- |

| | | | |
| --- | --- | --- | --- |
| **ayudar a mi hermano** | *help my brother* | **ir al parque** | *go to the park* |
| **estudiar** | *study* | **jugar con mis amigos** | *play with my friends* |
| **hacer los deberes** | *do my homework* | **salir con mis amigos** | *go out with my friends* |

| ¿Qué hiciste ayer después del colegio? | What did you do yesterday after school? |
| --- | --- |

### PAST (PRETERITE)

| Ayer | *Yesterday* | **El viernes pasado** | *Last Friday* | **La semana pasada** | *Last week* |
| --- | --- | --- | --- | --- | --- |

| | |
| --- | --- |
| **arreglé el salón** | *I tidied the living room* |
| **ayudé a mi hermano** | *I helped my brother* |
| **comí en un restaurante chino** | *I ate in a Chinese restaurant* |
| **compré material escolar** | *I bought school equipment* |
| **di un paseo** | *I went for a walk* |
| **fui al estadio** | *I went to the stadium* |
| **hice footing en el parque** | *I went jogging in the park* |
| **leí un libro** | *I read a book* |
| **toqué la guitarra** | *I played the guitar* |
| **salí con mi mejor amigo/a** | *I went out with my best friend* |

| ¿Qué planes tienes para este fin de semana? | What plans do you have for this weekend? |
| --- | --- |

### FUTURE (IMMEDIATE)

| El próximo fin de semana | *Next weekend* | **La próxima semana** | *Next week* | **Mañana** | *Tomorrow* |
| --- | --- | --- | --- | --- | --- |

| | | | |
| --- | --- | --- | --- |
| | | **arreglar mi dormitorio** | *tidy my room* |
| **(No) Quiero** | *I (don't) want to* | **ayudar en casa** | *help at home* |
| **(No) Me gustaría** | *I would (not) like to* | **hacer mis deberes** | *do my homework* |
| **(No) Tengo que** | *I (don't) have to* | **ir al cine** | *go to the cinema* |
| **(No) Voy a** | *I'm (not) going to* | **quedar con mis amigos** | *meet up with my friends* |
| | | **tocar el ukelele** | *play the ukulele* |

# UNIT 3 – FIND SOMEONE WHO – Student Cards

| | | | |
|---|---|---|---|
| Entre semana hago mis deberes y arreglo el salón.<br><br>**PEPE** | Por lo general monto en bici. Suelo ir al parque.<br><br>**XAVI** | El viernes pasado fui al estadio y ayudé en casa.<br><br>**JAMES** | El viernes pasado toqué la guitarra.<br><br>**PACO** |
| Por lo general arreglo mi habitación.<br><br>**NANCY** | El próximo fin de semana quiero quedar con mis amigos.<br><br>**MARÍA** | El fin de semana juego a la Play. El próximo fin de semana voy a tocar el ukelele.<br>**ARTURO** | Ayer di un paseo. Me gusta salir con mis amigos.<br><br>**ALEJANDRO** |
| Mañana tengo que ayudar en casa. Ayer ayudé a mi hermano.<br><br>**JULIA** | Tengo que ir al parque. Suelo jugar con mis amigos.<br><br>**DAVID** | El próximo fin de semana no quiero arreglar mi habitación.<br><br>**AMELIA** | La semana pasada hice footing en el parque. Me gusta ir al parque.<br><br>**ASUNCIÓN** |
| Suelo hacer los deberes entre semana. Mañana no quiero hacer mis deberes.<br>**JACOBO** | El fin de semana como en un restaurante. Mañana me gustaría quedar con mis amigos.<br>**MARIE** | Ayer salí con mi mejor amigo. La semana pasada di un paseo.<br><br>**JORGE** | Por lo general voy al centro comercial. La próxima semana voy a ir al cine.<br>**JUANFRAN** |

# UNIT 3 – FIND SOMEONE WHO – Student Grid

| | **¿Qué haces en tu tiempo libre?** | *What do you do in your free time?* |
|---|---|---|
| **Find someone who...** | | **Name(s)** |
| **1.** | ...went to the stadium last Friday. | |
| **2.** | ...talks about tidying their room. | |
| **3.** | ...tidies the living room during the week. | |
| **4.** | ...rides a bike regularly. | |
| **5.** | ...usually does homework during the week. | |
| **6.** | ...likes to go to the park or out with friends. | |
| **7.** | ...talks about playing a musical instrument. | |
| **8.** | ...wants to meet up with friends next weekend. | |
| **9.** | ...helped their brother yesterday. | |
| **10.** | ...is going to the cinema next week. | |
| **11.** | ...went out with their best friend yesterday. | |
| **12.** | ...has to go to the park. | |
| **13.** | ...would like to meet up with friends tomorrow. | |

# UNIT 3 – ORAL PING-PONG – Person A

| ENGLISH | SPANISH | ENGLISH | SPANISH |
|---|---|---|---|
| **What do you normally do in your free time?** | ¿Qué haces normalmente en tu tiempo libre? | **During the week, I play with my brother.** | Entre semana juego con mi hermano. |
| **At the weekend, I go out with my boyfriend.** | | **I have to help my brother.** | |
| **Yesterday, I ate at a Chinese restaurant.** | Ayer comí en un restaurante chino. | **Last Friday, I bought school equipment.** | El viernes pasado compré material escolar. |
| **Last Friday, I played guitar.** | | **Next week, I would like to meet up with my friends.** | |
| **Tomorrow I am going to go to the cinema.** | Mañana voy a ir al cine. | **In general, I go to the shopping mall.** | Por lo general voy al centro comercial. |
| **In general, I ride my bike.** | | **I like to play with my friends.** | |
| **I usually go out with my friends.** | Suelo salir con mis amigos. | **What did you do yesterday after school?** | ¿Qué hiciste ayer después del colegio? |
| **What plans do you have for this weekend?** | | **Next weekend, I want to help at home.** | |
| **Next weekend, I don't want to do my homework.** | El próximo fin de semana no quiero hacer mis deberes. | **Yesterday, I went for a walk.** | Ayer di un paseo. |
| **Last week, I went to the stadium.** | | **Last week, I tidied the living room.** | |

# UNIT 3 – ORAL PING-PONG – Person B

| ENGLISH | SPANISH | ENGLISH | SPANISH |
|---|---|---|---|
| What do you normally do in your free time? | | During the week, I play with my brother. | |
| At the weekend, I go out with my boyfriend. | El fin de semana salgo con mi novio. | I have to help my brother. | Tengo que ayudar a mi hermano. |
| Yesterday, I ate at a Chinese restaurant. | | Last Friday, I bought school equipment. | |
| Last Friday, I played guitar. | El viernes pasado toqué la guitarra. | Next week, I would like to meet up with my friends. | La próxima semana me gustaría quedar con mis amigos. |
| Tomorrow I am going to go to the cinema. | | In general, I go to the shopping mall. | |
| In general, I ride my bike. | Por lo general monto en bici. | I like to play with my friends. | Me gusta jugar con mis amigos. |
| I usually go out with my friends. | | What did you do yesterday after school? | |
| What plans do you have for this weekend? | ¿Qué planes tienes para este fin de semana? | Next weekend, I want to help at home. | El próximo fin de semana quiero ayudar en casa. |
| Next weekend, I don't want to do my homework. | | Yesterday, I went for a walk. | |
| Last week, I went to the stadium. | La semana pasada fui al estadio. | Last week, I tidied the living room. | La semana pasada arreglé el salón. |

# No Snakes No Ladders

**START**

1. Last week, I played the guitar.
2. Next weekend, I have to help at home.
3. What do you normally do in your free time?
4. Next week, I don't want to go to the cinema.
5. Last Friday, I went for a walk.
6. Yesterday, I helped my brother.
7. In general, I play on the PlayStation.
8. During the week, I go out with my boyfriend.
9. In general, I eat at a restaurant.
10. Last Friday, I went out with my best friend.
11. I like to play with my friends.
12. Tomorrow I would like to meet up with my friends.
13. I usually go to the park.
14. Next week, I have to do my homework.
15. During the week, I help my parents.
16. What did you do yesterday after school?
17. At the weekend, I am going to go to the mall.
18. Yesterday I went to the stadium.
19. I have to go out with my friends.
20. Tomorrow I am going to meet up with my friends.
21. Yesterday, I read a book.
22. Next week, I would like to play the ukulele.
23. What plans do you have for this weekend?
24. During the week, I ride my bike.
25. Last week, I ate at a Chinese restaurant.
26. Tomorrow I am not going to tidy my room.
27. In general, I go out with my girlfriend.
28. I like to go to the park.
29. Next week, I don't want to play the ukulele.
30. Last Friday, I ate at a Chinese restaurant.

**FINISH**

# No Snakes No Ladders

| | | | | | | | |
|---|---|---|---|---|---|---|---|
| **SALIDA** | **1**<br>La semana pasada toqué la guitarra. | **2**<br>El próximo fin de semana tengo que ayudar en casa. | **3**<br>¿Qué haces normalmente en tu tiempo libre? | **4**<br>La próxima semana no quiero ir al cine. | **5**<br>El viernes pasado di un paseo. | **6**<br>Ayer ayudé a mi hermano. | **7**<br>Por lo general juego a la Play. |
| **15**<br>Entre semana ayudo a mis padres. | **14**<br>La próxima semana tengo que hacer mis deberes. | **13**<br>Suelo ir al parque. | **12**<br>Mañana me gustaría quedar con mis amigos. | **11**<br>Me gusta jugar con mis amigos. | **10**<br>El viernes pasado salí con mi mejor amigo/a. | **9**<br>Por lo general como en un restaurante. | **8**<br>Entre semana salgo con mi novio. |
| **16**<br>¿Qué hiciste ayer después del colegio? | **17**<br>El fin de semana voy al centro comercial. | **18**<br>Ayer fui al estadio. | **19**<br>Tengo que salir con mis amigos. | **20**<br>Mañana voy a quedar con mis amigos. | **21**<br>Ayer leí un libro. | **22**<br>La próxima semana me gustaría tocar el ukelele. | **23**<br>¿Qué planes tienes para este fin de semana? |
| **LLEGADA** | **30**<br>El viernes pasado comí en un restaurante chino. | **29**<br>La próxima semana no quiero tocar el ukelele. | **28**<br>Me gusta ir al parque. | **27**<br>Por lo general salgo con mi novia. | **26**<br>Mañana no voy a arreglar mi dormitorio. | **25**<br>La semana pasada comí en un restaurante chino. | **24**<br>Entre semana monto en bici. |

# UNIT 3 – STAIRCASE TRANSLATION

At the weekend, I go to the shopping mall.

At the weekend, I go to the shopping mall and I eat in a restaurant.

At the weekend, I go to the shopping mall and I eat in a restaurant. I usually go out with my friends.

At the weekend, I go to the shopping mall and I eat in a restaurant. I usually go out with my friends. Yesterday, I went jogging in the park.

At the weekend, I go to the shopping mall and I eat in a restaurant. I usually go out with my friends. Yesterday, I went jogging in the park. What did you do yesterday after school?

At the weekend, I go to the shopping mall and I eat in a restaurant. I usually go out with my friends. Yesterday, I went jogging in the park. What did you do yesterday after school? Next weekend, I have to help at home.

**Translate the last step here:**

#  UNIT 3 – FASTER! 

**Say:**

1. In general, I help my parents.

2. At the weekend, I do my homework.

3. I like to play with my friends.

4. Last week, I went jogging in the park.

5. During the week, I ride my bike.

6. I usually go to the park.

7. Next weekend, I don't want to go to the cinema.

8. Tomorrow I have to tidy my room.

9. Last Friday, I ate in a Chinese restaurant.

10. Next week, I'm going to play the ukelele.

|   | Time | Mistakes | Referee's name |
|---|------|----------|----------------|
| 1 |      |          |                |
| 2 |      |          |                |
| 3 |      |          |                |
| 4 |      |          |                |

# UNIT 3 – INFORMATION GAP TASK

Use these questions to find out the missing information from your partner. Answer the questions in the first person wherever you can: e.g. *Como en un restaurante....*

| | | |
|---|---|---|
| **¿Con qué frecuencia** __________ **?** <br> *How often__________?* <br><br> **¿Con quién** ________ **?** <br> *Who ____________ with?* | **...te arreglas tu habitación?** <br> **...comes en un restaurante?** <br> **...haces los deberes?** <br> **...das un paseo?** <br> **...tocas la guitarra?** <br> **...vas al parque?** <br> **...montas en bici?** | *...do you tidy your room?* <br> *...do you eat in a restaurant?* <br> *...do you do your homework?* <br> *...do you go for a walk?* <br> *...do you play the guitar?* <br> *...do you go to the park?* <br> *...do you ride your bike?* |

## PARTNER 1

| | Activity | How often | Who with |
|---|---|---|---|
| **Imogen** | | | My parents |
| **Henry** | Do homework | Next week | |
| **Zoe** | | | My friends |
| **Grace** | Ride my bike | During the week | |
| **Mia** | | | On my own |
| **Olivia** | | | |
| **Elsie** | Go for a walk | Yesterday | My best friend |

## PARTNER 2

| | Activity | How often | Who with |
|---|---|---|---|
| **Imogen** | Eat in a restaurant | At the weekend | |
| **Henry** | | | My sister |
| **Zoe** | Play guitar | Last week | |
| **Grace** | | | My parents |
| **Mia** | Tidy my room | Last Friday | |
| **Olivia** | Go to the park | Usually | My family |
| **Elsie** | | | |

# UNIT 3 – COMMUNICATIVE DRILLS

| 1 | 2 | 3 |
|---|---|---|
| **What did you do yesterday after school?**<br><br>- Yesterday, I went out with my best friend. And you?<br><br>**After school, I went for a walk and went to the stadium.**<br><br>- Tomorrow, I'd like to go to the stadium. | **What do you normally do in your free time?**<br><br>- In general, I play on the PlayStation. I play with my brother. What plans do you have for next weekend?<br><br>**Next weekend, I have to tidy my room.** | **Do you like to go to the park?**<br><br>- I like to go to the park and go out with friends too. And you?<br><br>**Yes. I like to. Tomorrow I want to meet up with my friends.**<br><br>- Tomorrow I'm going to the cinema with my parents. |
| 4 | 5 | 6 |
| **What plans do you have for next week?**<br><br>- Next week, I have to do my homework and help at home. I don't want to do my homework.<br><br>**Tomorrow I'm going to do my homework.** | **What do you normally do in your free time?**<br><br>- I usually play with my friends.<br><br>**What did you do yesterday?**<br><br>- Yesterday, I bought school equipment and read a book with my best friend Maria. | **At the weekend, I go out with my boyfriend. What do you do at the weekend?**<br><br>- I like to go to the park but tomorrow I have to help at home.<br><br>**This weekend, I don't want to help at home.**<br><br>- I want to meet up with my friends! |
| 7 | 8 | 9 |
| **Last Friday, I played the guitar with my brother. What did you do last Friday?**<br><br>- I helped my brother and I tidied the living room.<br><br>**And yesterday?**<br><br>- Yesterday, I went jogging in the park. | **What do you normally do during the week?**<br><br>- During the week, I usually go out with my friends.<br><br>**What plans do you have for tomorrow?**<br><br>- Tomorrow, I'd like to go to the cinema and play the ukulele. | **What did you do last Friday?**<br><br>- I usually do my homework but last Friday, I went to the stadium. And you?<br><br>**Last Friday, I went to the stadium too. Yesterday, I tidied the living room.**<br><br>- Very good. |

# UNIT 3 – COMMUNICATIVE DRILLS
## REFEREE CARD



| 1 | 2 | 3 |
|---|---|---|
| **¿Qué hiciste ayer después del colegio?**<br><br>- Ayer salí con mi mejor amigo. ¿Y tú?<br><br>**Después del colegio di un paseo y fui al estadio.**<br><br>- Mañana me gustaría ir al estadio. | **¿Qué haces normalmente en tu tiempo libre?**<br><br>- Por lo general juego a la Play. Juego con mi hermano. ¿Qué planes tienes para el próximo fin de semana?<br><br>**El próximo fin de semana tengo que arreglar mi dormitorio.** | **¿Te gusta ir al parque?**<br><br>- Me gusta ir al parque y salir con amigos también. ¿Y tú?<br><br>**Sí. Me gusta. Mañana quiero quedar con mis amigos.**<br><br>- Mañana voy a ir al cine con mis padres. |
| **4** | **5** | **6** |
| **¿Qué planes tienes para la próxima semana?**<br><br>- La próxima semana tengo que hacer mis deberes y ayudar en casa. No quiero hacer mis deberes.<br><br>**Mañana voy a hacer mis deberes.** | **¿Qué haces normalmente en tu tiempo libre?**<br><br>- Suelo jugar con mis amigos.<br><br>**¿Qué hiciste ayer?**<br><br>- Ayer compré material escolar y leí un libro con mi mejor amiga María. | **El fin de semana salgo con mi novio. ¿Qué haces en el fin de semana?**<br><br>- Me gusta ir al parque, pero mañana tengo que ayudar en casa.<br><br>**Este fin de semana no quiero ayudar en casa.**<br><br>- ¡Quiero quedar con mis amigos! |
| **7** | **8** | **9** |
| **El viernes pasado toqué la guitarra con mi hermano. ¿Qué hiciste el viernes pasado?**<br><br>- Ayudé a mi hermano y arreglé el salón.<br><br>**¿Y ayer?**<br><br>- Ayer hice footing en el parque. | **¿Qué haces normalmente entre semana?**<br><br>- Entre semana suelo salir con mis amigos.<br><br>**¿Qué planes tienes para mañana?**<br><br>- Mañana me gustaría ir al cine y tocar el ukelele. | **¿Qué hiciste el viernes pasado?**<br><br>- Suelo hacer mis deberes, pero el viernes pasado fui al estadio. ¿Y tú?<br><br>**El viernes pasado fui al estadio también. Ayer arreglé el salón.**<br><br>- Muy bien. |

# UNIT 3 – SURVEY

| | ¿Cómo te llamas?<br>*What is your name?* | ¿Qué haces normalmente en tu tiempo libre?<br>*What do you normally do in your free time?* | ¿Qué haces entre semana?<br>*What do you do during the week?* | ¿Qué hiciste ayer después del colegio?<br>*What did you do yesterday after school?* | ¿Qué planes tienes para este fin de semana?<br>*What plans do you have for this weekend?* | ¿Qué planes tienes para mañana?<br>*What plans do you have for tomorrow?* |
|---|---|---|---|---|---|---|
| *e.g.* | *Me llamo Juan.* | *Por lo general voy al centro comercial.* | *Entre semana hago mis deberes.* | *Ayer di un paseo.* | *Este fin de semana voy a ayudar en casa.* | *Mañana quiero ir al cine.* |
| **1.** | | | | | | |
| **2.** | | | | | | |
| **3.** | | | | | | |
| **4.** | | | | | | |
| **5.** | | | | | | |
| **6.** | | | | | | |
| **7.** | | | | | | |

# UNIT 3 – ANSWERS

## FIND SOMEONE WHO

| Find someone who… | | Name(s) |
|---|---|---|
| **1.** | …went to the stadium last Friday. | **James** |
| **2.** | …talks about tidying their room. | **Nancy/Amelia** |
| **3.** | …tidies the living room during the week. | **Pepe** |
| **4.** | …rides a bike regularly. | **Xavi** |
| **5.** | …usually does homework during the week. | **Jacobo** |
| **6.** | …likes to go to the park or out with friends. | **Asunción/Alejandro** |
| **7.** | …talks about playing a musical instrument. | **Paco/Arturo** |
| **8.** | …wants to meet up with friends next weekend. | **María** |
| **9.** | …helped their brother yesterday. | **Julia** |
| **10.** | …is going to the cinema next week. | **Juanfran** |
| **11.** | …went out with their best friend yesterday. | **Jorge** |
| **12.** | …has to go to the park. | **David** |
| **13.** | …would like to meet up with friends tomorrow. | **Marie** |

## STAIRCASE TRANSLATION

El fin de semana voy al centro comercial y como en un restaurante. Suelo salir con mis amigos. Ayer hice footing en el parque. ¿Qué hiciste ayer después del colegio? El próximo fin de semana tengo que ayduar en casa.

## FASTER!

**REFEREE SOLUTION:**

1. Por lo general ayudo a mis padres.
2. El fin de semana hago mis deberes.
3. Me gusta jugar con mis amigos.
4. La semana pasada hice footing en el parque.
5. Entre semana monto en bici.
6. Suelo ir al parque.
7. El próximo fin de semana no quiero ir al cine.
8. Mañana tengo que arreglar mi dormitorio.
9. El viernes pasado comí en un restaurante chino.
10. La próximo semana voy a tocar el ukelele.

## INFORMATION GAP TASK

| | Activity | How often | Who with |
|---|---|---|---|
| **Imogen** | Eat in a restaurant | At the weekend | My parents |
| **Henry** | Do homework | Next week | My sister |
| **Zoe** | Play guitar | Last week | My friends |
| **Grace** | Ride my bike | During the week | My parents |
| **Mia** | Tidy my room | Last Friday | On my own |
| **Olivia** | Go to the park | Usually | My family |
| **Elsie** | Go for a walk | Yesterday | My best friend |

# UNIT 4.
## Describing a typical day at school

| | |
|---|---|
| ¿A qué hora empiezan/terminan las clases? | *What time do lessons start/finish?* |
| ¿Qué clases tienes por la mañana? | *What lessons do you have in the morning?* |
| ¿Qué haces después del colegio? | *What do you do after school?* |
| ¿Qué reglas hay en tu colegio? | *What rules are there in your school?* |

| | | | | | |
|---|---|---|---|---|---|
| **El recreo es** | *Breaktime is* | | **las dos** | **las siete** | **de la mañana** |
| **Charlo con mis amigos** | *I chat to my friends* | | **las tres** | **las ocho** | *in the morning* |
| **La hora de comer es** | *Lunchtime is* | | **las cuatro** | **las nueve** | |
| **Las clases empiezan** | *Lessons start* | **a** | **las cinco** | **las diez** | **de la tarde** |
| **Las clases terminan** | *Lessons end* | *at* | **las seis** | **las once** | *in the afternoon* |
| **Llego al colegio** | *I get to school* | | | | |
| **Salgo del colegio** | *I leave school* | | **las siete y media** | *seven thirty* | |
| **Vuelvo a casa** | *I go back home* | | **las ocho y cuarto** | *quarter past eight* | |
| **Tengo la primera clase** | *I have my first class* | | **mediodía** | *midday/noon* | |

| | | | | | |
|---|---|---|---|---|---|
| **A primera hora** | *First lesson* | | | **español** | *Spanish* |
| **A segunda hora** | *Second lesson* | **tengo clase de** | | **inglés** | *English* |
| **A última hora** | *Last lesson* | *I have ... class* | | **matemáticas** | *maths* |

| | | | |
|---|---|---|---|
| **(No) Me gusta** *I (don't) like* | **el francés** *French* <br> **la historia** *history* | **porque (no) es** *because it is (not)* | **divertido/a** *fun* <br> **fácil** *easy* |

| | | | |
|---|---|---|---|
| **Después del colegio** *After school* | **hago** *I do* | **actividades extraescolares** <br> **mis deberes en la biblioteca** | *after school activities* <br> *my homework in the library* |
| | **voy al club de ajedrez** | *I go to chess club* | |

| **En mi colegio** *At my school* | | **hay algunas reglas** *there are some rules* | |
|---|---|---|---|
| | | **comer chicle** | *eat chewing gum* |
| | | **comer en las aulas** | *eat in the classrooms* |
| **(no) se debe** *one must (not)* <br> **(no) se puede** *one can (not)* | | **correr por los pasillos** | *run in the corridors* |
| | | **fumar** | *smoke* |
| | | **hacer cola en la cantina** | *queue up in the canteen* |
| **tienes que** *you have to* <br> **no tienes que** *you don't have to* | | **ir al baño durante las clases** | *go to the toilet during lessons* |
| | | **levantar la mano antes de hablar** | *raise one's hand before speaking* |
| | | **usar/utilizar el móvil** | *use the mobile phone* |
| **(no) debo** *I must (not)* <br> **(no) puedo** *I can (not)* | | **auriculares** | *headphones* |
| | | **faldas cortas** | *short skirts* |
| | | **faldas largas** | *long skirts* |
| | **llevar** *wear* | **maquillaje** | *make-up* |
| **tengo que** *I have to* <br> **no tengo que** *I don't have to* | | **pendientes** | *earrings* |
| | | **uniforme** | *uniform* |
| | | **zapatillas** | *trainers* |

**THE LANGUAGE GYM**
SPEAKING BOOKLET III

# UNIT 4 – FIND SOMEONE WHO – Student Cards

| | | | |
|---|---|---|---|
| La hora de comer es a mediodía.<br><br>**JULIO** | A primera hora tengo clase de inglés.<br><br>**LUCÍA** | Me gusta el español porque es fácil.<br><br>**FELICIANO** | En mi colegio no se debe fumar.<br><br>**JESÚS** |
| A segunda hora tengo clase de matemáticas.<br><br>**MIGUEL** | Después del colegio hago mis deberes en la biblioteca.<br><br>**JUANA** | Llego al colegio a las ocho de la mañana.<br><br>**MÍA** | En mi colegio tienes que llevar uniforme.<br><br>**MARTINA** |
| En mi colegio no se puede comer chicle.<br><br>**ALEXIS** | A última hora tengo clase de español.<br><br>**KARINA** | El recreo es a las diez de la mañana.<br><br>**JORGE** | Vuelvo a casa a las tres de la tarde.<br><br>**JOSÉ** |
| En mi colegio se puede ir al baño durante las clases.<br><br>**CARLA** | Las clases empiezan a las nueve de la mañana.<br><br>**CARLITOS** | Salgo del colegio a las dos de la tarde.<br><br>**ANTONIO** | Después del colegio voy al club de ajedrez.<br><br>**ALBA** |

# UNIT 4 – FIND SOMEONE WHO – Student Grid

| ¿A qué hora empiezan/terminan las clases? | *What time do lessons start/finish?* |
|---|---|
| ¿Qué clases tienes por la mañana? | *What lessons do you have in the morning?* |
| ¿Qué haces después del colegio? | *What do you do after school?* |
| ¿Qué reglas hay en tu colegio? | *What rules are there in your school?* |

| | Find someone who... | Name(s) |
|---|---|---|
| 1. | ...has English class first thing in the morning. | |
| 2. | ...likes Spanish because it is easy. | |
| 3. | ...must wear uniform at their school. | |
| 4. | ...has maths second lesson. | |
| 5. | ...goes home at 3:00 in the afternoon. | |
| 6. | ...does an activity after school. | |
| 7. | ...cannot eat chewing gum or smoke at their school. | |
| 8. | ...arrives at school at 8:00 in the morning. | |
| 9. | ...says that lunch is at midday. | |
| 10. | ...says that breaktime is at 10:00 in the morning. | |
| 11. | ...says that lessons start at 9:00 in the morning. | |
| 12. | ...leaves school at 2:00 in the afternoon. | |
| 13. | ...has Spanish last lesson. | |
| 14. | ...is allowed to go to the toilet during lessons. | |

# UNIT 4 – ORAL PING-PONG – Person A

| ENGLISH | SPANISH | ENGLISH | SPANISH |
|---|---|---|---|
| Lessons start at 8:00 in the morning. | Las clases empiezan a las ocho de la mañana. | At my school, there are some rules. | En mi colegio hay algunas reglas. |
| Last lesson I have Spanish class. | | One must not use the mobile phone. | |
| After school, I do after school activities. | Después del colegio hago actividades extraescolares. | Second lesson I have maths class. | A segunda hora tengo clase de matemáticas. |
| At my school, one cannot eat in the classrooms. | | At my school, I cannot wear earrings. | |
| I like English because it is fun. | Me gusta el inglés porque es divertido. | After school, I do my homework in the library. | Después del colegio hago mis deberes en la biblioteca. |
| I leave school at 6:00 in the afternoon. | | At my school, I must not wear short skirts. | |
| Breaktime is at 11:00 in the morning. | El recreo es a las once de la mañana. | Lessons end at 4:00 in the afternoon. | Las clases terminan a las cuatro de la tarde. |
| What lessons do you have in the morning? | | What do you do after school? | |
| I have my first lesson at 7:00 in the morning. | Tengo la primera clase a las siete de la mañana. | Lunchtime is at 2:00 in the afternoon. | La hora de comer es a las dos de la tarde. |
| At my school, one must not run in the corridors. | | I go back home at 5:00 in the afternoon. | |

# UNIT 4 – ORAL PING-PONG – Person B

| ENGLISH | SPANISH | ENGLISH | SPANISH |
|---|---|---|---|
| Lessons start at 8:00 in the morning. | | At my school, there are some rules. | |
| Last lesson I have Spanish class. | A última hora tengo clase de español. | One must not use the mobile phone. | No se debe utilizar el móvil. |
| After school, I do after school activities. | | Second lesson I have maths class. | |
| At my school, one cannot eat in the classrooms. | En mi colegio no se puede comer en las aulas. | At my school, I cannot wear earrings. | En mi colegio no puedo llevar pendientes. |
| I like English because it is fun. | | After school, I do my homework in the library. | |
| I leave school at 6:00 in the afternoon. | Salgo del colegio a las seis de la tarde. | At my school, I must not wear short skirts. | En mi colegio no debo llevar faldas cortas. |
| Breaktime is at 11:00 in the morning. | | Lessons end at 4:00 in the afternoon. | |
| What lessons do you have in the morning? | ¿Qué clases tienes por la mañana? | What do you do after school? | ¿Qué haces después del colegio? |
| I have my first lesson at 7:00 in the morning. | | Lunchtime is at 2:00 in the afternoon. | |
| At my school, one must not run in the corridors | En mi colegio no se debe correr en los pasillos. | I go back home at 5:00 in the afternoon. | Vuelvo a casa a las cinco de la tarde. |

# No Snakes No Ladders

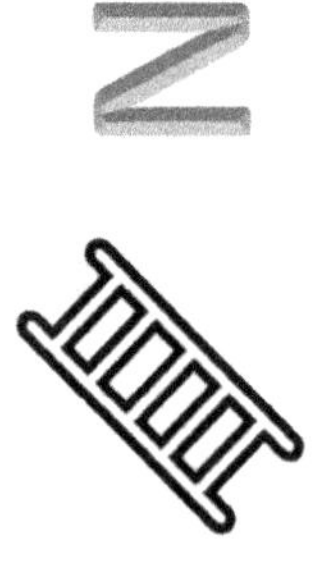

| | | | |
|---|---|---|---|
| **7** What time do lessons start? | **8** First lesson I have Spanish class. | **23** I have my first lesson at 9:00 in the morning. | **24** Last lesson I have maths class. |
| **6** Last lesson I have English class. | **9** At my school, you have to raise one's hand before speaking. | **22** What lessons do you have in the morning? | **25** What lessons do you have in the afternoon? |
| **5** At my school, one must not wear trainers. | **10** Breaktime is at 10:00 in the morning. | **21** One must not use the mobile phone. | **26** At my school, one can eat in the classrooms. |
| **4** After school, I do my homework in the library. | **11** At my school, one cannot wear make-up. | **20** At my school, I must not smoke. | **27** Lessons end at 3:00 in the afternoon. |
| **3** I like Spanish because it is fun. | **12** After school, I chat to my friends. | **19** I don't like English because it's easy. | **28** After school, I go to chess club. |
| **2** I go back home at 6:00 in the afternoon. | **13** I arrive at school at 7:00 in the morning. | **18** At my school, I have to wear long skirts. | **29** At my school, I have to wear uniform. |
| **1** Lessons start at 8:00 in the morning. | **14** Lunchtime is at 2:00 in the afternoon. | **17** At my school, there are some rules. | **30** Second lesson I have English class. |
| START | **15** What rules are there in your school? | **16** I leave school at 4:00 in the afternoon. | FINISH |

# UNIT 4

# No Snakes No Ladders

| | | | |
|---|---|---|---|
| **7** ¿A qué hora empiezan las clases? | **8** A primera hora tengo clase de español. | **23** Tengo la primera clase a las nueve de la mañana. | **24** A última hora tengo clase de matemáticas. |
| **6** A última hora tengo clase de inglés. | **9** En mi colegio tienes que levantar la mano antes de hablar. | **22** ¿Qué clases tienes por la mañana? | **25** ¿Qué clases tienes por la tarde? |
| **5** En mi colegio no se debe llevar zapatillas. | **10** El recreo es a las diez de la mañana. | **21** No se debe utilizar el móvil. | **26** En mi colegio se puede comer en las aulas. |
| **4** Después del colegio hago mis deberes en la biblioteca. | **11** En mi colegio no se puede llevar maquillaje. | **20** En mi colegio no debo fumar. | **27** Las clases terminan a las tres de la tarde. |
| **3** Me gusta el español porque es divertido. | **12** Después del colegio charlo con mis amigos. | **19** No me gusta el inglés porque es fácil. | **28** Después del colegio voy al club de ajedrez. |
| **2** Vuelvo a casa a las seis de la tarde. | **13** Llego al colegio a las siete de la mañana. | **18** En mi colegio tengo que llevar faldas largas. | **29** En mi colegio tengo que llevar uniforme. |
| **1** Las clases empiezan a las ocho de la mañana. | **14** La hora de comer es a las dos de la tarde. | **17** En mi colegio hay algunas reglas. | **30** A segunda hora tengo clase de inglés. |
| **SALIDA** | **15** ¿Qué reglas hay en tu colegio? | **16** Salgo del colegio a las cuatro de la tarde. | **LLEGADA** |

# UNIT 4 – STAIRCASE TRANSLATION

I get to school at 7:00 in the morning and lessons start at 8:00.

I get to school at 7:00 in the morning and lessons start at 8:00. I have my first class at 9:00

I get to school at 7:00 in the morning and lessons start at 8:00. I have my first class at 9:00. First lesson I have English class.

I get to school at 7:00 in the morning and lessons start at 8:00. I have my first class at 9:00. First lesson I have English class. Second lesson I have Spanish class. I like Spanish because it is fun.

I get to school at 7:00 in the morning and lessons start at 8:00. I have my first class at 9:00. First lesson I have English class. Second lesson I have Spanish class. I like Spanish because it is fun. Lunchtime is at midday. After school, I do my homework in the library.

I get to school at 7:00 in the morning and lessons start at 8:00. I have my first class at 9:00. First lesson I have English class. Second lesson I have Spanish class. I like Spanish because it is fun. Lunchtime is at midday. After school, I do my homework in the library. At my school, one cannot eat in the classrooms and you have to wear uniform.

**Translate the last step here:**

#  UNIT 4 – FASTER! 

## Say:

1. First lesson I have Spanish class.

2. Lessons end at 4:00 in the afternoon.

3. At my school, there are some rules.

4. After school, I do after school activities.

5. Breaktime is at 11:00 in the morning.

6. At my school, you have to queue up in the canteen.

7. What lessons do you have in the morning?

8. I like maths because it is easy.

9. I go back home at 6:00 in the afternoon.

10. At my school, I must not wear headphones.

|   | Time | Mistakes | Referee's name |
|---|------|----------|----------------|
| 1 |      |          |                |
| 2 |      |          |                |
| 3 |      |          |                |
| 4 |      |          |                |

# UNIT 4 – THINGS IN COMMON

Write your own answers to the questions then interview four friends and make a note of what things you have in common.

| | Yo<br>*(Your own answer)* | 1 | 2 | 3 | 4 |
|---|---|---|---|---|---|
| **¿A qué hora empiezan las clases?** | | | | | |
| **¿Qué clases tienes por la mañana?** | | | | | |
| **¿Qué clases tienes por la tarde?** | | | | | |
| **¿A qué hora es el recreo?** | | | | | |
| **¿A qué hora es la hora de comer?** | | | | | |
| **¿Te gusta el español?** | | | | | |
| **¿Qué reglas hay en tu colegio?** | | | | | |
| **¿Qué haces después del colegio?** | | | | | |
| **¿A qué hora vuelves a casa?** | | | | | |

# UNIT 4 – COMMUNICATIVE DRILLS

| 1 | 2 | 3 |
|---|---|---|
| **What lessons do you have in the morning?**<br><br>- First lesson I have English class.<br><br>**And second lesson?**<br><br>- Second lesson I have Spanish class. I like Spanish because it's fun. | **What rules are there in your school?**<br><br>- At my school, there are some rules. One cannot smoke and one must not use the mobile phone. And you?<br><br>**At my school, you have to wear uniform and wear long skirts. I don't like it.** | **What do you do after school?**<br><br>- Classes end at 3:00 in the afternoon and I go back home at 5:00.<br><br>**After school, I go to chess club and I chat to my friends.**<br><br>- I like chess too! |
| **4** | **5** | **6** |
| **I have my first lesson at 8:00 in the morning. And you? What time do lessons start?**<br><br>- Lessons start at 9:00 in the morning.<br><br>**What lesson do you have first lesson?**<br><br>- First lesson I have maths class. | **At my school, one cannot wear earrings.**<br><br>- At my school, one cannot wear make-up.<br><br>**What do you do after school?**<br><br>- After school, I do my homework in the library. | **What rules are there in your school?**<br><br>- At my school, one must not go to the toilet during lessons and one must raise one's hand before speaking.<br><br>**At my school, one can use the mobile phone.**<br><br>- How good! |
| **7** | **8** | **9** |
| **What time do lessons start?**<br><br>- Lessons start at 10:00 in the morning.<br><br>**What time do lessons finish?**<br><br>- Lessons end at 3:00 and I go back home. | **What time do you have breaktime?**<br><br>- Breaktime is at 11:00 in the morning. And you?<br><br>**There are two. At 10:00 in the morning and at 2:00 in the afternoon.**<br><br>- I go back home at 2:00 in the afternoon! | **What class do you have last lesson?**<br><br>- Last lesson I have Spanish class.<br><br>**Do you like Spanish?**<br><br>- I like Spanish because it's easy. I don't like English. |

# UNIT 4 – COMMUNICATIVE DRILLS
## REFEREE CARD

| 1 | 2 | 3 |
|---|---|---|
| **¿Qué clases tienes por la mañana?**<br><br>- A primera hora tengo clase de inglés.<br><br>**¿Y a segunda hora?**<br><br>- A segunda hora tengo clase de español. Me gusta el español porque es divertido. | **¿Qué reglas hay en tu colegio?**<br><br>- En mi colegio hay algunas reglas. No se puede fumar y no se debe utilizar el móvil. ¿Y tú?<br><br>**En mi colegio tienes que llevar uniforme y llevar faldas largas. No me gusta.** | **¿Qué haces después del colegio?**<br><br>- Las clases terminan a las tres de la tarde y vuelvo a casa a las cinco.<br><br>**Después del colegio voy al club de ajedrez y charlo con mis amigos.**<br><br>- ¡Me gusta el ajedrez también! |

| 4 | 5 | 6 |
|---|---|---|
| **Tengo la primera clase a las ocho de la mañana. ¿Y tú? ¿A qué hora empiezan las clases?**<br><br>- Las clases empiezan a las nueve de la mañana.<br><br>**¿Qué clase tienes a primera hora?**<br><br>- A primera hora tengo clase de matemáticas. | **En mi colegio no se puede llevar pendientes.**<br><br>- En mi colegio no se puede llevar maquillaje.<br><br>**¿Qué haces después del colegio?**<br><br>- Después del colegio hago mis deberes en la biblioteca. | **¿Qué reglas hay en tu colegio?**<br><br>- En mi colegio no se debe ir al baño durante las clases y se debe levantar la mano antes de hablar.<br><br>**En mi colegio se puede utilizar el móvil.**<br><br>- ¡Qué bien! |

| 7 | 8 | 9 |
|---|---|---|
| **¿A qué hora empiezan las clases?**<br><br>- Las clases empiezan a las diez de la mañana.<br><br>**¿A qué hora terminan las clases?**<br><br>- Las clases terminan a las tres y vuelvo a casa. | **¿A qué hora tienes el recreo?**<br><br>- El recreo es a las once de la mañana. ¿Y tú?<br><br>**Hay dos. A las diez de la mañana y a las dos de la tarde.**<br><br>- ¡Vuelvo a casa a las dos de la tarde! | **¿Qué clase tienes a última hora?**<br><br>- A última hora tengo clase de español.<br><br>**¿Te gusta el español?**<br><br>- Me gusta el español porque es fácil. No me gusta el inglés. |

# UNIT 4 – SURVEY

| | ¿Cómo te llamas?<br>*What is your name?* | ¿A qué hora empiezan las clases?<br>*What time do lessons start?* | ¿A qué hora terminan las clases?<br>*What time do lessons finish?* | ¿Qué clases tienes por la mañana?<br>*What lessons do you have in the morning?* | ¿Qué haces después del colegio?<br>*What do you do after school?* | ¿Qué reglas hay en tu colegio?<br>*What rules are there in your school?* |
|---|---|---|---|---|---|---|
| *e.g.* | *Me llamo Juan.* | *Las clases empiezan a las ocho de la mañana.* | *Las clases terminan a las tres de la tarde.* | *A primera hora tengo clase de inglés.* | *Después del colegio hago actividades extraescolares.* | *En mi colegio no se puede comer chicle.* |
| 1. | | | | | | |
| 2. | | | | | | |
| 3. | | | | | | |
| 4. | | | | | | |
| 5. | | | | | | |
| 6. | | | | | | |
| 7. | | | | | | |

# UNIT 4 – ANSWERS

## FIND SOMEONE WHO

| Find someone who... | | Name(s) |
|---|---|---|
| **1.** | ...has English class first thing in the morning. | **Lucía** |
| **2.** | ...likes Spanish because it is easy. | **Feliciano** |
| **3.** | ...must wear uniform at their school. | **Martina** |
| **4.** | ...has maths second lesson. | **Miguel** |
| **5.** | ...goes home at 3:00 in the afternoon. | **José** |
| **6.** | ...does an activity after school. | **Juana/Alba** |
| **7.** | ...cannot eat chewing gum or smoke at their school. | **Alexis/Jesús** |
| **8.** | ...arrives at school at 8:00 in the morning. | **Mía** |
| **9.** | ...says that lunch is at midday. | **Julio** |
| **10.** | ...says that breaktime is at 10:00 in the morning. | **Jorge** |
| **11.** | ...says that lessons start at 9:00 in the morning. | **Carlitos** |
| **12.** | ...leaves school at 2:00 in the afternoon. | **Antonio** |
| **13.** | ...has Spanish last lesson. | **Karina** |
| **14.** | ...is allowed to go to the toilet during lessons. | **Carla** |

## STAIRCASE TRANSLATION

Llego al colegio a las siete de la mañana y las clases empiezan a las ocho. Tengo la primera clase a las nueve. A primera hora tengo clase de inglés. A segunda hora tengo clase de español. Me gusta el español porque es divertido. La hora de comer es a mediodía. Después del colegio hago mis deberes en la biblioteca. En mi colegio no se puede comer en las aulas y tienes que llevar uniforme.

## FASTER!

**REFEREE SOLUTION:**
1. A primera hora tengo clase de español.
2. Las clases terminan a las cuatro de la tarde.
3. En mi colegio hay algunas reglas.
4. Después del colegio hago actividades extraescolares.
5. El recreo es a las once de la mañana.
6. En mi colegio tienes que hacer cola en la cantina.
7. ¿Qué clases tienes por la mañana?
8. Me gustan las matemáticas porque son fáciles.
9. Vuelvo a casa a las seis de la tarde.
10. En mi colegio no debo llevar auriculares.

## THINGS IN COMMON

Students give their own answers to the questions and make a note of which students they have things in common with.

# UNIT 5.
## Talking about when I went to *La Tomatina*

| ¿Has ido a alguna fiesta típica española? | *Have you ever been to any typical Spanish festival?* |
|---|---|
| ¿Cuándo fuiste? / ¿Qué hiciste? / ¿Cómo fue? | *When did you go? / What did you do? / How was it?* |

| El fin de semana pasado | fui | con | mi mejor amigo/a | *my best friend* | a Buñol |
|---|---|---|---|---|---|
| *Last weekend* | *I went* | *with* | mis amigos | *my friends* | *to Buñol* |

| para participar en | *to take part in* | la Tomatina |
|---|---|---|

| Viajé | *I travelled* | en | avión | *plane* | y luego | en | autocar | *coach* |
|---|---|---|---|---|---|---|---|---|
| Viajamos | *We travelled* | | coche | *car* | *and then* | | tren | *train* |

| El viaje fue *The trip was* | corto *short* | largo *long* | pero *but* | y *and* | divertido *fun* | duro *hard* |
|---|---|---|---|---|---|---|

| Cuando *When* | llegué | *I arrived* | alquilé | *I rented* | un coche *a car* |
|---|---|---|---|---|---|
| | llegamos | *we arrived* | alquilamos | *we rented* | |

| El día de la fiesta | me desperté | *I woke up* | a las ocho | *at 8* |
|---|---|---|---|---|
| *On the day of the festival* | mi amigo/a se despertó | *my friend woke up* | muy temprano | *very early* |
| | nos despertamos | *we woke up* | | |

| Luego *Then* | llegué | temprano *early* | al pueblo | para coger sitio |
|---|---|---|---|---|
| | llegamos | | *to the town* | *to get a good spot* |

| Por la mañana *In the morning,* | hizo buen/mal tiempo | | *the weather was good/bad* |
|---|---|---|---|
| pero luego *but later* | hizo *it was* | calor/frío/sol | *hot/cold/sunny* |
| | estuvo nublado | | *it was cloudy* |
| Por la tarde *In the afternoon,* | hubo tormenta | | *it was stormy* |
| | llovió un poco | | *it rained a bit* |

| Durante la batalla de tomates | conocí /conocimos | *I/we met* | a mucha gente | *many people* |
|---|---|---|---|---|
| | me caí / nos caímos | *I/we fell over* | muchas veces | *many times* |
| *During the tomato fight,* | tiré / tiramos | *I/we threw* | un montón de tomates | *loads of tomatoes* |
| | me ensucié / nos ensuciamos | *I/we got dirty* | mucho *a lot* | |
| | me reí / nos reímos | *I/we laughed* | | |

| Después de la fiesta | volví | al hotel | y | comí tapas | *I ate tapas* | comimos tapas | *we ate tapas* |
|---|---|---|---|---|---|---|---|
| *After the festival,* | *I returned* | | | descansé | *I rested* | descansamos | *we rested* |
| | volvimos *we returned* | | | me duché | *I showered* | nos duchamos | *we showered* |

| Finalmente *Finally,* | me acosté *I went to bed* | a las | diez. | Fue una experiencia *It was a(n)... experience* | increíble | *incredible* |
|---|---|---|---|---|---|---|
| | nos acostamos *we went to bed* | | | | inolvidable | *unforgettable* |
| | | | | | maravillosa | *marvellous* |

| En esta fiesta hay algunas reglas importantes | *In this festival there are some important rules* |
|---|---|

| Solo se debe | *One must only* | tirar *throw* | tomates | *tomatoes* |
|---|---|---|---|---|
| No se debe | *One must not* | | botellas | *bottles* |
| Nunca se debe | *One must never* | | piedras | *stones* |

| Además, *Furthermore,* | es una buena idea *it's a good idea* | llevar *to wear* | gafas de natación | *swimming goggles* |
|---|---|---|---|---|
| | se recomienda *it's recommended* | | camisetas viejas | *old T-shirts* |
| | | | zapatillas | *trainers* |

# UNIT 5 – FIND SOMEONE WHO – Student Cards

| | | | |
|---|---|---|---|
| El día de la fiesta me desperté muy temprano.<br><br>**ANTONIO** | Cuando llegué alquilé un coche.<br><br>**PEPA** | Viajé en avión y luego en tren.<br><br>**DOLORES** | Durante la batalla de tomates me reí mucho.<br><br>**ALMA** |
| El viaje fue corto pero divertido.<br><br>**MIRABEL** | Después de la fiesta volví al hotel y descansé.<br><br>**PEPE** | En esta fiesta solo se debe tirar tomates.<br><br>**JULIETA** | Por la tarde llovió un poco.<br><br>**FELIX** |
| El fin de semana pasado fui con mis amigos a Buñol.<br><br>**ISABELLA** | Por la mañana estuvo nublado.<br><br>**BRUNO** | Durante la batalla tiré un montón de tomates.<br><br>**MARIANO** | Finalmente me acosté a las diez.<br><br>**ARTURO** |
| No se debe tirar piedras. Es una buena idea llevar gafas de natación.<br><br>**LUISA** | Después de la fiesta volvimos al hotel y comimos tapas.<br><br>**CAMILO** | Viajé en coche. El viaje fue largo y duro.<br><br>**AGUSTÍN** | Durante la batalla de tomates conocí a mucha gente.<br><br>**OSVALDO** |

# UNIT 5 – FIND SOMEONE WHO – Student Grid

| ¿Has ido a alguna fiesta típica española? ¿Cuándo fuiste? / ¿Qué hiciste? / ¿Cómo fue? | *Have you ever been to any typical Spanish festival? When did you go? / What did you do? / How was it?* |
|---|---|

| | Find someone who... | Name(s) |
|---|---|---|
| **1.** | ...travelled by plane and then by train. | |
| **2.** | ...travelled by or rented a car. | |
| **3.** | ...thought the journey was short but fun. | |
| **4.** | ...woke up very early on the day of the festival. | |
| **5.** | ...met a lot of people during the tomato fight. | |
| **6.** | ...said it rained a bit in the afternoon. | |
| **7.** | ...laughed a lot during the tomato fight. | |
| **8.** | ...returned to the hotel after the festival. | |
| **9.** | ...said it was cloudy in the morning. | |
| **10.** | ...went to Buñol with friends last weekend. | |
| **11.** | ...mentions throwing tomatoes. | |
| **12.** | ...went to bed at 10:00. | |
| **13.** | ...says that you should not throw stones. | |

# UNIT 5 – ORAL PING-PONG – Person A

| ENGLISH | SPANISH | ENGLISH | SPANISH |
|---|---|---|---|
| I travelled by plane and then by coach. | Viajé en avión y luego en autocar. | During the tomato fight, I fell over many times. | Durante la batalla de tomates me caí muchas veces. |
| On the day of the festival, we woke up at 8:00. | | Have you ever been to any typical Spanish festival? | |
| Then we arrived early to the town to get a good spot. | Luego llegamos temprano al pueblo para coger sitio. | In the afternoon, it was hot. | Por la tarde hizo calor. |
| During the fight I got very dirty. | | It was a marvellous experience. | |
| Furthermore, it's a good idea to wear old t-shirts. | Además, es una buena idea llevar camisetas viejas. | One must never throw bottles. | Nunca se debe tirar botellas. |
| After the festival, I returned to the hotel and I showered. | | Finally, we went to bed at 10:00. | |
| When we arrived, we rented a car. | Cuando llegamos alquilamos un coche. | Furthermore, it is recommended to wear trainers. | Además, se recomienda llevar zapatillas. |
| In the morning, the weather was good. | | In this festival, there are some important rules. | |
| The journey was long but fun. | El viaje fue largo pero divertido. | I went with my friends to take part in la Tomatina. | Fui con mis amigos para participar en la Tomatina. |
| Last weekend, I went with my best friend to Buñol. | | When did you go? How was it? | |

# UNIT 5 – ORAL PING-PONG – Person B

| ENGLISH | SPANISH | ENGLISH | SPANISH |
|---|---|---|---|
| I travelled by plane and then by coach. | | During the tomato fight, I fell over many times. | |
| On the day of the festival, we woke up at 8:00. | El día de la fiesta nos despertamos a las ocho. | Have you ever been to any typical Spanish festival? | ¿Has ido a alguna fiesta típica española? |
| Then we arrived early to the town to get a good spot. | | In the afternoon, it was hot. | |
| During the fight I got very dirty. | Durante la batalla me ensucié mucho. | It was a marvellous experience. | Fue una experiencia maravillosa. |
| Furthermore, it's a good idea to wear old t-shirts. | | One must never throw bottles. | |
| After the festival, I returned to the hotel and I showered. | Después de la fiesta volví al hotel y me duché. | Finally, we went to bed at 10:00. | Finalmente nos acostamos a las diez. |
| When we arrived, we rented a car. | | Furthermore, it is recommended to wear trainers. | |
| In the morning, the weather was good. | Por la mañana hizo buen tiempo. | In this festival, there are some important rules. | En esta fiesta hay algunas reglas importantes. |
| The journey was long but fun. | | I went with my friends to take part in la Tomatina. | |
| Last weekend, I went with my best friend to Buñol. | El fin de semana pasado fui con mi mejor amigo/a a Buñol. | When did you go? How was it? | ¿Cuándo fuiste? ¿Cómo fue? |

# No Snakes No Ladders

|  |  |
|---|------|
| START | |
| 1 | On the day of the festival, I woke up very early. |
| 2 | Then we arrived early to the town to get a good spot. |
| 3 | I travelled by plane and then by car. |
| 4 | In the morning, it was cold. |
| 5 | In this festival there are some important rules. |
| 6 | One must only throw tomatoes. |
| 7 | Finally, I went to bed at 10:00. |
| 8 | What did you do? |
| 9 | When we arrived we rented a car. |
| 10 | In the afternoon, the weather was good. |
| 11 | During the tomato fight, I laughed a lot. |
| 12 | Furthermore, it is recommended to wear swimming goggles. |
| 13 | Last weekend, I went with my friends to Buñol. |
| 14 | It was an unforgettable experience. |
| 15 | On the day of the festival, my friend woke up at 8:00. |
| 16 | After the festival, I returned to the hotel and I ate tapas. |
| 17 | The journey was short and fun. |
| 18 | During the tomato fight, I got dirty. |
| 19 | Have you ever been to any typical Spanish festival? |
| 20 | In the morning, it was sunny… |
| 21 | …but in the afternoon it was cloudy. |
| 22 | How was it? When did you go? |
| 23 | The journey was long and hard. |
| 24 | I went with my best friend to take part in la Tomatina. |
| 25 | After the festival, we returned to the hotel and we rested. |
| 26 | It was an unforgettable experience. |
| 27 | In the afternoon, it was stormy. |
| 28 | One must not throw stones. |
| 29 | Furthermore, it is a good idea to wear trainers. |
| 30 | During the tomato fight, I fell over many times. |
| FINISH | |

# No Snakes No Ladders

| | | | |
|---|---|---|---|
| **7** Finalmente me acosté a las diez. | **8** ¿Qué hiciste? | **23** El viaje fue largo y duro. | **24** Fui con mi mejor amigo/a para participar en la Tomatina. |
| **6** Solo se debe tirar tomates. | **9** Cuando llegamos alquilamos un coche. | **22** ¿Cómo fue? ¿Cuándo fuiste? | **25** Después de la fiesta volvimos al hotel y descansamos. |
| **5** En esta fiesta hay algunas reglas importantes. | **10** Por la tarde hizo buen tiempo. | **21** ...pero por la tarde estuvo nublado. | **26** Fue una experiencia inolvidable. |
| **4** Por la mañana hizo frío. | **11** Durante la batalla de tomates me reí mucho. | **20** Por la mañana hizo sol... | **27** Por la tarde hubo tormenta. |
| **3** Viajé en avión y luego en coche. | **12** Además, se recomienda llevar gafas de natación. | **19** ¿Has ido a alguna fiesta típica española? | **28** No se debe tirar piedras. |
| **2** Luego llegamos temprano al pueblo para coger sitio. | **13** El fin de semana pasado fui con mis amigos a Buñol. | **18** Durante la batalla de tomates me ensucié. | **29** Además, es una buena idea llevar zapatillas. |
| **1** El día de la fiesta me desperté muy temprano. | **14** Fue una experiencia inolvidable. | **17** El viaje fue corto y divertido. | **30** Durante la batalla de tomates me caí muchas veces. |
| **SALIDA** | **15** El día de la fiesta mi amigo/a se despertó a las ocho. | **16** Después de la fiesta volví al hotel y comí tapas. | **LLEGADA** |

# UNIT 5 – STAIRCASE TRANSLATION

Last weekend, I went with my best friend to Buñol.

Last weekend, I went with my best friend to Buñol to take part in la Tomatina.

Last weekend, I went with my best friend to Buñol to take part in la Tomatina. We travelled by plane and then by coach.

Last weekend, I went with my best friend to Buñol to take part in la Tomatina. We travelled by plane and then by coach. On the day of the festival, I woke up very early.

Last weekend, I went with my best friend to Buñol to take part in la Tomatina. We travelled by plane and then by coach. On the day of the festival, I woke up very early. During the tomato fight, I met many people and I laughed.

Last weekend, I went with my best friend to Buñol to take part in la Tomatina. We travelled by plane and then by coach. On the day of the festival, I woke up very early. During the tomato fight, I met many people and I laughed. After the festival, we returned to the hotel and we rested.

**Translate the last step here:**

#  UNIT 5 – FASTER! 

**Say:**

1. Have you ever been to any typical Spanish festival?

2. Last weekend, I went to take part in la Tomatina.

3. I travelled by car and then by train.

4. What did you do during the festival?

5. During the tomato fight, we threw loads of tomatoes.

6. After the festival, I returned to the hotel and I ate tapas.

7. Finally, we went to bed at 10:00. It was an incredible experience.

8. In this festival, there are some important rules.

|   | Time | Mistakes | Referee's name |
|---|------|----------|----------------|
| 1 |      |          |                |
| 2 |      |          |                |
| 3 |      |          |                |
| 4 |      |          |                |

# UNIT 5 – FAST & FURIOUS 

## ROUND 1

### (Verbs in 1st person singular)

1. El fin de semana pasado *I went* con mis amigos a Buñol.
2. *I travelled* en avión y luego en tren.
3. Cuando *I arrived, I rented* un coche.
4. El día de la fiesta *I woke up* muy temprano.
5. Luego *I arrived* temprano al pueblo para coger sitio.
6. Durante la batalla de tomates *I met* a mucha gente.
7. *I threw* un montón de tomates.
8. Después de la fiesta *I returned* al hotel y *I rested*.
9. Finalmente *I went to bed* a las diez.

|  | Time 1 | Time 2 | Time 3 | Time 4 |
|---|---|---|---|---|
| **Time** |  |  |  |  |
| **Mistakes** |  |  |  |  |

## ROUND 2

### (Verbs in 1st person plural)

1. El fin de semana pasado *we went* a Buñol.
2. *We travelled* en avión y luego en tren.
3. Cuando *we arrived, we rented* un coche.
4. El día del festival *we woke up* muy temprano.
5. Luego *we arrived* temprano al pueblo para coger sitio.
6. Durante la batalla de tomates *we met* a mucha gente.
7. *We threw* un montón de tomates.
8. Después de la fiesta *we returned* al hotel y *we rested*.
9. Finalmente *we went to bed* at ten.

|  | Time 1 | Time 2 | Time 3 | Time 4 |
|---|---|---|---|---|
| **Time** |  |  |  |  |
| **Mistakes** |  |  |  |  |

# UNIT 5 – COMMUNICATIVE DRILLS

| 1 | 2 | 3 |
|---|---|---|
| **When did you go to Spain?**<br><br>- Last weekend, I went with my friends to Buñol.<br><br>**Why?**<br><br>- To participate in la Tomatina. We travelled by plane and then by train. | **Have you ever been to a typical Spanish festival?**<br><br>- I went with my best friend to take part in la Tomatina!<br><br>**How was it?**<br><br>It was an amazing experience. During the fight, I threw loads of tomatoes. | **In the morning it was cloudy.**<br><br>- And in the afternoon?<br><br>**In the afternoon, the weather was good. I got very dirty and after, I returned to the hotel and I showered.**<br><br>- When did you go?<br><br>**I went last weekend.** |
| 4 | 5 | 6 |
| **What did you do at the festival?**<br><br>- During the festival, I met a lot of people and we threw a lot of tomatoes.<br><br>**Are there rules?**<br><br>- Yes, there are some important rules. One must only throw tomatoes. | **How was the Tomatina?**<br><br>- It was a marvellous experience.<br><br>**What did you do in the morning?**<br><br>- In the morning, I woke up at 8:00 and I arrived early in the town to get a good spot. | **How was the trip?**<br><br>- I travelled by car and the trip was long but fun.<br><br>**What did you do after the festival?**<br><br>- After the festival, we went back to the hotel and we ate tapas. It was incredible! |
| 7 | 8 | 9 |
| **In this festival, there are some important rules.**<br><br>- What rules are there?<br><br>**One must not throw bottles and it's recommended to wear swimming goggles.**<br><br>- How was the festival?<br><br>**It was an unforgettable experience.** | **Did you go with your family?**<br><br>- No, I went with my best friend (f). When we arrived, we rented a car.<br><br>**What did you do at the festival?**<br><br>- During the tomato fight, I laughed a lot and we fell over many times. | **Have you ever been to a typical Spanish festival?**<br><br>-Yes. Last weekend, I went with my family to take part in la Tomatina in Buñol.<br><br>**How was it?**<br><br>- It was a marvellous experience. We met a lot of people. |

# UNIT 5 – COMMUNICATIVE DRILLS
## REFEREE CARD



| 1 | 2 | 3 |
|---|---|---|
| **¿Cuándo fuiste a España?**<br><br>- El fin de semana pasado fui con mis amigos a Buñol.<br><br>**¿Por qué?**<br><br>- Para participar en la Tomatina. Viajamos en avión y luego en tren. | **¿Has ido a alguna fiesta típica española?**<br><br>- ¡Fui con mi mejor amigo/a para participar en la Tomatina!<br><br>**¿Cómo fue?**<br><br>Fue una experiencia increíble. Durante la batalla tiré un montón de tomates. | Por la mañana estuvo nublado.<br><br>- ¿Y por la tarde?<br><br>**Por la tarde hizo buen tiempo. Me ensucié mucho y después volví al hotel y me duché.**<br><br>- ¿Cuándo fuiste?<br><br>**Fui el fin de semana pasado.** |

| 4 | 5 | 6 |
|---|---|---|
| **¿Qué hiciste en la fiesta?**<br><br>- Durante la fiesta conocí a mucha gente y tiramos muchos tomates.<br><br>**¿Hay reglas?**<br><br>- Sí, hay algunas reglas importantes. Solo se debe tirar tomates. | **¿Cómo fue la Tomatina?**<br><br>- Fue una experiencia maravillosa.<br><br>**¿Qué hiciste por la mañana?**<br><br>- Por la mañana me desperté a las ocho y llegué temprano al pueblo para coger sitio. | **¿Cómo fue el viaje?**<br><br>- Viajé en coche y el viaje fue largo pero divertido.<br><br>**¿Qué hiciste después de la fiesta?**<br><br>- Después de la fiesta volvimos al hotel y comimos tapas. ¡Fue increíble! |

| 7 | 8 | 9 |
|---|---|---|
| **En esta fiesta hay algunas reglas importantes.**<br><br>- ¿Qué reglas hay?<br><br>**No se debe tirar botellas y se recomienda llevar gafas de natación.**<br><br>- ¿Cómo fue la fiesta?<br><br>**Fue una experiencia inolvidable.** | **¿Fuiste con tu familia?**<br><br>- No, fui con mi mejor amiga. Cuando llegamos alquilamos un coche.<br><br>**¿Qué hiciste en la fiesta?**<br><br>- Durante la batalla de tomates me reí mucho y nos caímos muchas veces. | **¿Has ido a una fiesta típica española?**<br><br>- Sí. El fin de semana pasado fui con mi familia a participar en la Tomatina en Buñol.<br><br>**¿Cómo fue?**<br><br>- Fue una experiencia maravillosa. Conocimos a mucha gente. |

# UNIT 5 – SURVEY

| | ¿Cómo te llamas?<br>*What is your name?* | ¿Cómo viajaste a Buñol?<br>*How did you travel to Buñol?* | ¿Qué tiempo hizo?<br>*What was the weather like?* | ¿Qué hiciste?<br>*What did you do?* | ¿Qué hiciste después de la fiesta?<br>*What did you do after the festival?* | ¿Qué reglas hay?<br>*What rules are there?* |
|---|---|---|---|---|---|---|
| *e.g.* | *Me llamo Juan.* | *Viajé en coche y luego en tren.* | *Por la mañana hizo buen tiempo.* | *Durante la batalla de tomates me reí mucho.* | *Después de la fiesta volví al hotel y me duché.* | *Nunca se debe tirar piedras.* |
| **1.** | | | | | | |
| **2.** | | | | | | |
| **3.** | | | | | | |
| **4.** | | | | | | |
| **5.** | | | | | | |
| **6.** | | | | | | |
| **7.** | | | | | | |

# UNIT 5 – ANSWERS

## FIND SOMEONE WHO

| Find someone who... | | Name(s) |
|---|---|---|
| **1.** | ...travelled by plane and then by train. | **Dolores** |
| **2.** | ...travelled by or rented a car. | **Pepa/Agustín** |
| **3.** | ...thought the journey was short but fun. | **Mirabel** |
| **4.** | ...woke up very early on the day of the festival. | **Antonio** |
| **5.** | ...met a lot of people during the tomato fight. | **Osvaldo** |
| **6.** | ...said it rained a bit in the afternoon. | **Felix** |
| **7.** | ...laughed a lot during the tomato fight. | **Alma** |
| **8.** | ...returned to the hotel after the festival. | **Camilo/Pepe** |
| **9.** | ...said it was cloudy in the morning. | **Bruno** |
| **10.** | ...went to Buñol with friends last weekend. | **Isabella** |
| **11.** | ...mentions throwing tomatoes. | **Mariano/Julieta** |
| **12.** | ...went to bed at 10:00. | **Arturo** |
| **13.** | ...says that you should not throw stones. | **Luisa** |

## STAIRCASE TRANSLATION

El fin de semana pasado fui con mi mejor amigo/a a Buñol para participar en la Tomatina. Viajamos en avión y luego en autocar. El día de la fiesta me desperté muy temprano. Durante la batalla de tomates conocí a mucha gente y me reí. Después de la fiesta volvimos al hotel y descansamos.

## FASTER!

**REFEREE SOLUTION:**

1. ¿Has ido a alguna fiesta típica española?

2. El fin de semana pasado fui para participar en la Tomatina.

3. Viajé en coche y luego en tren.

4. ¿Qué hiciste durante la fiesta?

5. Durante la batalla de tomates tiramos un montón de tomates.

6. Después de la fiesta volví al hotel y comí tapas.

7. Finalmente nos acostamos a las diez. Fue una experiencia increíble.

8. En esta fiesta hay algunas reglas importantes.

## FAST & FURIOUS

**ROUND 1**

1. El fin de semana pasado **fui** con mis amigos a Buñol.
2. **Viajé** en avión y luego en tren.
3. Cuando **llegué alquilé** un coche.
4. El día de la fiesta **me desperté** muy temprano.
5. Luego **llegué** temprano al pueblo para coger sitio.

6. Durante la batalla de tomates **conocí** a mucha gente.
7. **Tiré** un montón de tomates.
8. Después de la fiesta **volví** al hotel y **descansé**.
9. Finalmente **me acosté** a las diez.

**ROUND 2**

1. El fin de semana pasado **fuimos** a Buñol.
2. **Viajamos** en avión y luego en tren.
3. Cuando **llegamos alquilamos** un coche.
4. El día de la fiesta **nos despertamos** muy temprano.
5. Luego **llegamos** temprano al pueblo para coger sitio.

6. Durante la batalla de tomates **conocimos** a mucha gente.
7. **Tiramos** un montón de tomates.
8. Después de la fiesta **volvimos** al hotel y **descansamos**.
9. Finalmente **nos acostamos** a las diez.

# UNIT 6.
## Talking about yesterday after school

| ¿A qué hora te levantaste ayer? | *What time did you get up yesterday?* |
| ¿Cómo fuiste al colegio? | *How did you go to school?* |
| ¿Qué hiciste ayer cuando volviste a casa? | *What did you do yesterday when you got home?* |

| **Ayer** *Yesterday* | **por la mañana** *(in the) morning* | **me levanté** *I got up* <br> **desayuné** *I had breakfast* <br> **fui al colegio** *I went to school* | **a las seis/siete** *at six/seven* |

| **En el colegio** *At school* | **tuve clase de** *I had a ... lesson* | **español** **francés** | **y** | **aprendí mucho** *I learnt a lot* <br> **fue divertido** *it was fun* <br> **lo pasé bien/mal** *I had a good/bad time* |

| **Luego** *Later* | **volví a casa** *I returned home* | **a las tres** *at 3:00* | **a pie** *on foot* <br> **en autobús** *by bus* <br> **en coche** *by car* |

| **Durante el viaje a casa** *During the trip home* | **dormí** *I slept* <br> **escuché música** *I listened to music* <br> **hablé con mis amigos/as** *I talked to my friends* |

| **Cuando llegué a casa** *When I got home* | **hice los deberes** *I did my homework* <br> **jugué a la Switch** *I played on my Switch* <br> **jugué a videojuegos** *I played video games* <br> **saqué al perro** *I took the dog out* <br> **toqué el piano** *I played the piano* | **en mi dormitorio** *in my bedroom* <br> **en el salón** *in the living room* <br> **en el jardín** *in the garden* |

| **Luego, por la tarde** *Later, in the afternoon* | **charlé con mis amigos** *I chatted with my friends* <br> **fui a casa de mi amigo** *I went to my friend's house* <br> **fui al parque** *I went to the park* <br> **quedé con mis amigos** *I met up with my friends* <br> **salí al centro comercial** *I went to the shopping mall* |

| **Después de cenar** *After dinner* | **me metí en internet** *I went on the internet* <br> **usé mi móvil** *I used my phone* <br> **usé mi portátil** *I used my laptop* | **para** *(in order) to* | **buscar información** *look for information* <br> **mirar mi Instagram** *look at my Insta* <br> **ver vídeos en YouTube** *watch videos on YouTube* |

# UNIT 6 – FIND SOMEONE WHO – Student Cards

| | | | |
|---|---|---|---|
| Ayer por la mañana me levanté a las seis.<br><br>**MIGUEL** | Durante el viaje a casa escuché música.<br><br>**ERNESTO** | Cuando llegué a casa hice los deberes en mi dormitorio.<br><br>**BERTO** | Después de cenar usé mi móvil para mirar mi Instagram.<br><br>**FRIDA** |
| Luego volví a casa a las tres en coche.<br><br>**IMELDA** | Luego, por la tarde fui a casa de mi amigo.<br><br>**JULIO** | En el colegio tuve clase de español y aprendí mucho.<br><br>**ROSA** | Ayer por la mañana fui al colegio a las siete.<br><br>**VICTORIA** |
| Después de cenar usé mi portátil para buscar información.<br><br>**OSCAR** | Durante el viaje a casa hablé con mis amigos.<br><br>**ROSITA** | Cuando llegué a casa saqué al perro en el jardín.<br><br>**HÉCTOR** | En el colegio tuve clase de francés y lo pasé mal.<br><br>**COCO** |
| Ayer por la mañana desayuné a las siete.<br><br>**FELIPE** | Luego, por la tarde fui a casa de mi amigo para jugar a videojuegos.<br><br>**ABEL** | Luego volví a casa a las tres a pie.<br><br>**JUAN** | Cuando llegué a casa jugué a videojuegos en el salón.<br><br>**GUSTAVO** |

# UNIT 6 – FIND SOMEONE WHO – Student Grid

| | |
|---|---|
| **¿A qué hora te levantaste ayer?** | *What time did you get up yesterday?* |
| **¿Cómo fuiste al colegio?** | *How did you go to school?* |
| **¿Qué hiciste ayer cuando volviste a casa?** | *What did you do yesterday when you got home?* |

| | Find someone who... | Name(s) |
|---|---|---|
| **1.** | ...went to a friend's house in the afternoon. | |
| **2.** | ...talked with friends during the journey home. | |
| **3.** | ...returned home at three by car or on foot. | |
| **4.** | ...used their mobile to check Instagram after dinner. | |
| **5.** | ...did homework in their bedroom when they got home. | |
| **6.** | ...woke up at six yesterday morning. | |
| **7.** | ...listened to music during the journey home. | |
| **8.** | ...used their laptop to search for information after dinner. | |
| **9.** | ...mentions what they did at seven yesterday morning. | |
| **10.** | ...had a Spanish lesson at school and learned a lot. | |
| **11.** | ...took the dog out in the garden when they got home. | |
| **12.** | ...had a French lesson at school and had a bad time. | |
| **13.** | ...played videogames when they got home. | |

# UNIT 6 – ORAL PING-PONG – Person A

| ENGLISH | SPANISH | ENGLISH | SPANISH |
|---|---|---|---|
| **Yesterday morning I went to school at 7:00.** | Ayer por la mañana fui al colegio a las siete. | **At school, I had a French lesson and I had a good time.** | En el colegio tuve clase de francés y lo pasé bien. |
| **During the journey home, I slept.** | | **Later, I returned home by car.** | |
| **Later, I returned home at 3:00 by bus.** | Luego volví a casa a las tres en autobús. | **After dinner, I used my phone to look at my Insta.** | Después de cenar usé mi móvil para mirar mi Instagram. |
| **When I got home, I did my homework in the living room.** | | **When I got home, I took the dog out in the garden.** | |
| **After dinner, I went on the internet to watch videos on YouTube.** | Después de cenar me metí en internet para ver vídeos en YouTube. | **Then, in the afternoon, I went to the park.** | Luego, por la tarde fui al parque. |
| **At school, I had a Spanish lesson and it was fun.** | | **During the journey home, I listened to music.** | |
| **Yesterday, I got up at 6:00.** | Ayer me levanté a las seis. | **How did you get to school?** | ¿Cómo fuiste al colegio? |
| **What time did you get up yesterday?** | | **What did you do yesterday when you got home?** | |
| **Later, in the afternoon, I chatted with my friends.** | Luego, por la tarde charlé con mis amigos. | **When I got home, I played video games in my bedroom.** | Cuando llegué a casa jugué a videojuegos en mi dormitorio. |
| **When I got home, I played the piano in my bedroom.** | | **Then, in the afternoon, I went to the shopping mall.** | |

# UNIT 6 – ORAL PING-PONG – Person B

| ENGLISH | SPANISH | ENGLISH | SPANISH |
|---|---|---|---|
| Yesterday morning I went to school at 7:00. | | At school, I had a French lesson and I had a good time. | |
| During the journey home, I slept. | Durante el viaje a casa dormí. | Later, I returned home by car. | Luego volví a casa en coche. |
| Later, I returned home at 3:00 by bus. | | After dinner, I used my phone to look at my Insta. | |
| When I got home, I did my homework in the living room. | Cuando llegué a casa hice los deberes en el salón. | When I got home, I took the dog out in the garden. | Cuando llegué a casa saqué al perro en el jardín. |
| After dinner, I went on the internet to watch videos on YouTube. | | Then, in the afternoon, I went to the park. | |
| At school, I had a Spanish lesson and it was fun. | En el colegio tuve clase de español y fue divertido. | During the journey home, I listened to music. | Durante el viaje a casa escuché música. |
| Yesterday, I got up at 6:00. | | How did you get to school? | |
| What time did you get up yesterday? | ¿A qué hora te levantaste ayer? | What did you do yesterday when you got home? | ¿Qué hiciste ayer cuando volviste a casa? |
| Later, in the afternoon, I chatted with my friends. | | When I got home, I played video games in my bedroom. | |
| When I got home, I played the piano in my bedroom. | Cuando llegué a casa toqué el piano en mi dormitorio. | Then, in the afternoon, I went to the shopping mall. | Luego, por la tarde salí al centro comercial. |

# UNIT 6

# No Snakes No Ladders

| | | | | | |
|---|---|---|---|---|---|
| **7**<br>At school, I had a French lesson and it was fun. | **6**<br>Yesterday morning, I got up at 6:00. | **5**<br>Later, I returned home at 3:00 by bus. | **4**<br>How did you get to school? | **3**<br>During the journey home, I listened to music. | **2**<br>Later, in the afternoon, I went to a friend's house. |
| **8**<br>When I got home, I played the piano in the living room. | **9**<br>After dinner, I used my phone to watch videos on YouTube. | **10**<br>Later, I returned home on foot. | **11**<br>What time did you go to school? | **12**<br>Later, in the afternoon, I met up with my friends. | **13**<br>When I got home, I took the dog out in the garden. |
| **23**<br>After dinner, I went on the internet to look at my Insta. | **22**<br>Later, in the afternoon, I went to the park. | **21**<br>Yesterday morning, I talked with my friends. | **20**<br>When I got home, I listened to music. | **19**<br>After dinner, I used my laptop to look for information. | **18**<br>What time did you return home? |
| **24**<br>During the journey to school, I did my homework. | **25**<br>Later, I returned home and took the dog out. | **26**<br>What did you do in the afternoon? | **27**<br>Yesterday, I used my phone to watch videos on YouTube. | **28**<br>At school, I chatted with my friends. | **29**<br>Later, in the afternoon, I chatted with my friends. |

| | |
|---|---|
| **1**<br>At school, I had a Spanish lesson and I learned a lot. | **15**<br>When I got home, I played video games in my bedroom. |
| **14**<br>Then, I returned home by car. | START |
| **17**<br>During the journey home, I chatted with my friends. | **16**<br>At school, I had a Spanish lesson and I had a good time. |
| **30**<br>After dinner, I went to my friend's house. | FINISH |

# No Snakes No Ladders

| | **1** En el colegio tuve clase de español y aprendí mucho. | **2** Luego, por la tarde fui a casa de un amigo/a. | **3** Durante el viaje a casa escuché música. | **4** ¿Cómo fuiste al colegio? | **5** Luego volví a casa a las tres en autobús. | **6** Ayer por la mañana me levanté a las seis. | **7** En el colegio tuve clase de francés y fue divertido. |
|---|---|---|---|---|---|---|---|
| **SALIDA** | | | | | | | |
| **15** Cuando llegué a casa jugué a videojuegos en mi dormitorio. | **14** Luego volví a casa en coche. | **13** Cuando llegué a casa saqué al perro en el jardín. | **12** Luego, por la tarde quedé con mis amigos/as. | **11** ¿A qué hora fuiste al colegio? | **10** Luego volví a casa a pie. | **9** Después de cenar usé mi móvil para ver vídeos en YouTube. | **8** Cuando llegué a casa toqué el piano en el salón. |
| **16** En el colegio tuve clase de español y lo pasé bien. | **17** Durante el viaje a casa charlé con mis amigos/as. | **18** ¿A qué hora volviste a casa? | **19** Después de cenar usé mi portátil para buscar información. | **20** Cuando llegué a casa escuché música. | **21** Ayer por la mañana hablé con mis amigos. | **22** Luego, por la tarde fui al parque. | **23** Después de cenar me metí en internet para mirar mi Instagram. |
| **LLEGADA** | **30** Después de cenar fui a casa de mi amigo/a. | **29** Luego, por la tarde charlé con mis amigos/as. | **28** En el colegio charlé con mis amigos/as. | **27** Ayer usé mi móvil para ver vídeos en YouTube. | **26** ¿Qué hiciste por la tarde? | **25** Luego volví a casa y saqué al perro. | **24** Durante el viaje al colegio hice los deberes. |

# UNIT 6 – STAIRCASE TRANSLATION

Yesterday morning, I got up at 6:00.

Yesterday morning, I got up at 6:00. At school, I had a Spanish lesson and I learnt a lot

Yesterday morning, I got up at 6:00. At school, I had a Spanish lesson and I learnt a lot. Later, I returned home at 3:00 by car.

Yesterday morning, I got up at 6:00. At school, I had a Spanish lesson and I learnt a lot. Later, I returned home at 3:00 by car. During the journey home, I listened to music. When I got home, I did my homework in the living room.

Yesterday morning, I got up at 6:00. At school, I had a Spanish lesson and I learnt a lot. Later, I returned home at 3:00 by car. During the journey home, I listened to music. When I got home, I did my homework in the living room. Later, in the afternoon, I met up with my friends.

Yesterday morning, I got up at 6:00. At school, I had a Spanish lesson and I learnt a lot. Later, I returned home at 3:00 by car. During the journey home, I listened to music. When I got home, I did my homework in the living room. Later, in the afternoon, I met up with my friends. After dinner, I used my phone to look at my Insta.

Translate the last step here:

 # UNIT 6 – FASTER! 

## Say:

1. What time did you get up yesterday?

2. Yesterday morning, I got up at 6:00.

3. At school, I had a French lesson and it was fun.

4. Later, I returned home at 3:00 by car.

5. What did you do yesterday when you got home?

6. When I got home, I played video games in my bedroom.

7. Later, I went to the shopping mall.

8. Later, in the afternoon, I chatted with my friends.

9. After dinner, I used my phone to watch videos on YouTube.

10. I used my laptop to look for information.

|   | Time | Mistakes | Referee's name |
|---|---|---|---|
| 1 |  |  |  |
| 2 |  |  |  |
| 3 |  |  |  |
| 4 |  |  |  |

# UNIT 6 – TRAPDOOR

| | | |
|---|---|---|
| Cuando llegué a casa<br>Luego, por la tarde<br>Después de cenar<br>Durante el viaje a casa | hice los deberes<br>jugué a videojuegos<br>toqué el piano<br>usé mi móvil<br>me metí en internet<br>fui al parque<br>escuché música<br>salí al centro comercial | con mis amigos<br>en mi dormitorio<br>en el salón<br>para buscar información<br>para mirar mi Instagram<br>en mi casa<br>en casa de un amigo/a |

1. When I got home, I played video games in my bedroom.
2. Later, in the afternoon, I went to the park with my friends.
3. After dinner, I went on the internet to look for information.
4. During the journey home, I listened to music.
5. When I got home, I used my phone to look at my Insta.
6. Later, in the afternoon, I played the piano in the living room.
7. After dinner, I did my homework at home.

|  | Time 1 | Time 2 | Time 3 | Time 4 |
|---|---|---|---|---|
| **Time** |  |  |  |  |
| **Mistakes** |  |  |  |  |

# UNIT 6 – COMMUNICATIVE DRILLS

| 1 | 2 | 3 |
|---|---|---|
| **How did you go to school?**<br><br>- I went by car. During the journey, I listened to music.<br><br>**What did you do when you got back home?**<br><br>- When I got home, I chatted with my friends. | **What time did you get up yesterday?**<br><br>- Yesterday morning, I got up at 7:00. And you?<br><br>**I got up at 6:00 and I had breakfast at 7:00. Did you go to the park?**<br><br>- Yes, I went with my friend. | **At school, I had a Spanish lesson and I had a good time. And you?**<br><br>- I had a bad time. I had a French lesson but when I got home, I played video games in the living room.<br><br>**Ah, very good.** |

| 4 | 5 | 6 |
|---|---|---|
| **What did you do yesterday afternoon?**<br><br>- In the afternoon, I met up with my friends and I went to the shopping mall. And you?<br><br>**After dinner, I used my phone to watch videos on YouTube.**<br><br>-Me too. | **During the journey home, I chatted with my friends. How did you get home?**<br><br>- I returned home at 3:00 on foot. What did you do when you got home?<br><br>**When I got home, I took the dog out in the garden. And you?**<br><br>- I chatted with my friends in my bedroom. | **What time did you get up yesterday?**<br><br>- Yesterday morning, I got up at 6:00 and used my laptop to look up information.<br><br>**I got up at 10:00!**<br><br>- How nice! |

| 7 | 8 | 9 |
|---|---|---|
| **How did you get home yesterday?**<br><br>- I returned home by bus with my friends.<br><br>**What did you do after dinner?**<br><br>- After dinner, I went on the internet to watch videos on YouTube. | **At school, I had a French lesson and I learnt a lot.**<br><br>- I went to school at 7:00 and had a Spanish lesson.<br><br>**What time did you return home?**<br><br>- I returned home in the afternoon at 4:00. | **What did you do during the journey home yesterday?**<br><br>- Yesterday, during the journey home, I slept.<br><br>**What time did you get up in the morning?**<br><br>- Yesterday morning, I got up at 5:00. |

# UNIT 6 – COMMUNICATIVE DRILLS
## REFEREE CARD



| 1 | 2 | 3 |
|---|---|---|
| **¿Cómo fuiste al colegio?**<br><br>- Fui en coche. Durante el viaje escuché música.<br><br>**¿Qué hiciste cuando volviste a casa?**<br><br>- Cuando llegué a casa charlé con mis amigos. | **¿A qué hora te levantaste ayer?**<br><br>- Ayer por la mañana me levanté a las siete. ¿Y tú?<br><br>**Me levanté a las seis y desayuné a las siete. ¿Fuiste al parque?**<br><br>- Sí, fui con mi amigo/a. | **En el colegio tuve clase de español y lo pasé bien. ¿Y tú?**<br><br>- Lo pasé mal. Tuve clase de francés, pero cuando llegué a casa jugué a videojuegos en el salón.<br><br>**Ah, muy bien.** |
| **4** | **5** | **6** |
| **¿Qué hiciste ayer por la tarde?**<br><br>- Por la tarde quedé con mis amigos y salí al centro comercial. ¿Y tú?<br><br>**Después de cenar usé mi móvil para ver vídeos en YouTube.**<br><br>- Yo también. | **Durante el viaje a casa charlé con mis amigos/as. ¿Cómo volviste a casa?**<br><br>- Volví a casa a las tres a pie. ¿Qué hiciste cuando volviste a casa?<br><br>**Cuando llegué a casa saqué al perro en el jardín. ¿Y tú?**<br><br>- Charlé con mis amigos/as en mi dormitorio. | **¿A qué hora te levantaste ayer?**<br><br>- Ayer por la mañana me levanté a las seis y usé mi portátil para buscar información.<br><br>**¡Me levanté a las diez!**<br><br>- ¡Qué bien! |
| **7** | **8** | **9** |
| **¿Cómo volviste a casa ayer?**<br><br>- Volví a casa en autobús con mis amigos/as.<br><br>**¿Qué hiciste después de cenar?**<br><br>- Después de cenar me metí en internet para ver vídeos en YouTube. | **En el colegio tuve clase de francés y aprendí mucho.**<br><br>- Fui al colegio a las siete y tuve clase de español.<br><br>**¿A qué hora volviste a casa?**<br><br>- Volví a casa por la tarde a las cuatro. | **¿Qué hiciste durante el viaje a casa ayer?**<br><br>- Ayer, durante el viaje a casa dormí.<br><br>**¿A qué hora te levantaste por la mañana?**<br><br>- Ayer por la mañana me levanté a las cinco. |

# UNIT 6 – SURVEY

| | ¿Cómo te llamas?<br>*What is your name?* | ¿A qué hora te levantaste ayer?<br>*What time did you get up yesterday?* | ¿Cómo volviste a casa ayer?<br>*How did you get home yesterday?* | ¿Qué hiciste durante el viaje a casa?<br>*What did you do during the journey home?* | ¿Qué hiciste ayer cuando volviste a casa?<br>*What did you do yesterday when you got home?* | ¿Qué hiciste después de cenar?<br>*What did you do after dinner?* |
|---|---|---|---|---|---|---|
| *e.g.* | *Me llamo Juan.* | *Ayer me levanté a las cinco.* | *Volví a casa en coche.* | *Durante el viaje a casa escuché música.* | *Cuando llegué a casa hice los deberes.* | *Después de cenar usé mi móvil para mirar mi Instagram.* |
| 1. | | | | | | |
| 2. | | | | | | |
| 3. | | | | | | |
| 4. | | | | | | |
| 5. | | | | | | |
| 6. | | | | | | |
| 7. | | | | | | |

# UNIT 6 – ANSWERS

## FIND SOMEONE WHO

| Find someone who... | | Name(s) |
|---|---|---|
| **1.** | ...went to a friend's house in the afternoon. | **Julio/Abel** |
| **2.** | ...talked with friends during the journey home. | **Rosita** |
| **3.** | ...returned home at three by car or on foot. | **Imelda/Juan** |
| **4.** | ...used their mobile to check Instagram after dinner. | **Frida** |
| **5.** | ...did homework in their bedroom when they got home. | **Berto** |
| **6.** | ...woke up at six yesterday morning. | **Miguel** |
| **7.** | ...listened to music during the journey home. | **Ernesto** |
| **8.** | ...used their laptop to search for information after dinner. | **Oscar** |
| **9.** | ...mentions what they did at seven yesterday morning. | **Victoria/Felipe** |
| **10.** | ...had a Spanish lesson at school and learned a lot. | **Rosa** |
| **11.** | ...took the dog out in the garden when they got home. | **Héctor** |
| **12.** | ...had a French lesson at school and had a bad time. | **Coco** |
| **13.** | ...played videogames when they got home. | **Gustavo** |

## STAIRCASE TRANSLATION

Ayer por la mañana me levanté a las seis. En el colegio tuve clase de español y aprendí mucho. Luego volví a casa a las tres en coche. Durante el viaje a casa escuché música. Cuando llegué a casa hice mis deberes en el salón. Luego, por la tarde quedé con mis amigos. Después de cenar usé mi móvil para mirar mi Instagram.

## FASTER!

**REFEREE SOLUTION:**

1. ¿A qué hora te levantaste ayer?
2. Ayer por la mañana me levanté a las seis.
3. En el colegio tuve clase de francés y fue divertido.
4. Luego volví a casa a las tres en coche.
5. ¿Qué hiciste ayer cuando llegaste a casa?
6. Cuando llegué a casa jugué a videojuegos en mi dormitorio.
7. Luego fui al centro comercial.
8. Luego, por la tarde charlé con mis amigos.
9. Después de cenar usé mi móvil para ver vídeos en YouTube.
10. Usé mi portátil para buscar información.

## TRAPDOOR

1. Cuando llegué a casa jugué a videojuegos en mi dormitorio.
2. Luego, por la tarde fui al parque con mis amigos/as.
3. Después de cenar me metí en internet para buscar información.
4. Durante el viaje a casa escuché música.
5. Cuando llegué a casa usé mi móvil para mirar mi Instagram.
6. Luego, por la tarde toqué el piano en el salón.
7. Después de cenar hice los deberes en casa.

# UNIT 7.
## Talking about where I went and what I did last weekend

| ¿Qué hiciste el fin de semana pasado? | *What did you do last weekend?* |
| --- | --- |
| ¿Qué hiciste el sábado/domingo? | *What did you do on Saturday/Sunday?* |
| ¿Qué hiciste antes de dormir? | *What did you do before going to sleep?* |

| El fin de semana pasado | fue | bastante | *quite* | divertido | *fun* |
| --- | --- | --- | --- | --- | --- |
| *Last weekend* | *was* | muy | *very* | entretenido | *entertaining* |

| Mis amigos y yo | fuimos a muchos sitios | *(we) went to many places* |
| --- | --- | --- |
| *My friends and I* | hicimos muchas cosas | *(we) did many things* |

| Por ejemplo, | fui | al centro comercial | | para | dar un paseo |
| --- | --- | --- | --- | --- | --- |
| *For example,* | *I went* | *to the shopping mall* | | | *go for a walk* |
| El viernes | fuimos | al centro de la ciudad | | *(in order) to* | mirar escaparates |
| *On Friday,* | *we went* | *to the city centre* | | | *go window shopping* |

| Y luego | fui | al cine | para ver una película | de acción | *action* |
| --- | --- | --- | --- | --- | --- |
| *And later* | fuimos | *to the cinema* | *to see a ... film* | nueva | *new* |
| | | | | de ciencia ficción | *sci-fi* |

| El sábado | pasé | un rato | buscando información | *looking for information* |
| --- | --- | --- | --- | --- |
| *On Saturday,* | *I spent* | *a while* | escuchando música | *listening to music* |
| | | una hora | estudiando español | *studying Spanish* |
| | | *an hour* | tocando la guitarra | *playing the guitar* |
| | | | usando el móvil | *using my mobile* |

| con mi amigo | *with my friend* | en mi | *in my* | casa | *house* |
| --- | --- | --- | --- | --- | --- |
| solo/sola | *alone* | | | dormitorio | *bedroom* |

| El domingo | no hice | mucho | porque | estaba cansado/a | *I was tired* |
| --- | --- | --- | --- | --- | --- |
| *On Sunday,* | *I didn't do* | *much* | *because* | estaba ocupado/a | *I was busy* |
| | | nada | | hacía mal tiempo | *the weather was bad* |
| | | *anything* | | tenía muchos deberes | *I had a lot of homework* |
| | | tanto | | | |
| | | *so much* | | | |

| Finalmente | me acosté | a | *at* | las nueve | *nine* |
| --- | --- | --- | --- | --- | --- |
| *Finally,* | *I went to bed* | a eso de | *at about* | las diez | *ten* |

| Antes de dormir | escuché un poco de música | *I listened to a bit of music* |
| --- | --- | --- |
| *Before going to sleep,* | hablé con mi amigo/a | *I spoke with my friend* |
| | leí mi libro | *I read my book* |

# UNIT 7 – FIND SOMEONE WHO – Student Cards

| | | | |
|---|---|---|---|
| Fui al centro comercial para mirar escaparates.<br><br>**JILL** | El sábado pasé un rato escuchando música.<br><br>**CESC** | Me acosté a eso de las diez.<br><br>**RAFAEL** | El domingo no hice mucho porque estaba ocupada.<br><br>**HELGA** |
| El viernes fuimos al centro de la ciudad para dar un paseo.<br><br>**ROCÍO** | El sábado pasé una hora estudiando español con mi amigo.<br><br>**JORDI** | El domingo no hice tanto porque hacía mal tiempo.<br><br>**MIKE** | Antes de dormir hablé con mi amigo.<br><br>**ISA** |
| Mis amigos y yo hicimos muchas cosas.<br><br>**JORGE** | Pasé un rato usando el móvil sola en mi dormitorio.<br><br>**CONCHITA** | Luego fui al cine para ver una película nueva.<br><br>**ÁLVARO** | Mis amigos y yo fuimos a muchos sitios.<br><br>**ÁNGEL** |
| El domingo fui al cine para ver una película nueva.<br><br>**MANOLO** | El viernes escuché un poco de música.<br><br>**YAMAL** | Luego pasé un rato tocando la guitarra en mi casa.<br><br>**NANCY** | El fin de semana pasado fue bastante entretenido.<br><br>**PAQUITO** |

# UNIT 7 – FIND SOMEONE WHO – Student Grid

| **¿Qué hiciste el fin de semana pasado?** | *What did you do last weekend?* |
|---|---|
| **¿Qué hiciste el sábado/domingo?** | *What did you do on Saturday/Sunday?* |
| **¿Qué hiciste antes de dormir?** | *What did you do before going to sleep?* |

| Find someone who... | | Name(s) |
|---|---|---|
| **1.** | ...spent some time using their phone alone in their bedroom. | |
| **2.** | ...spent some time playing the guitar at home. | |
| **3.** | ...went to the city centre to go for a walk on Friday. | |
| **4.** | ...didn't do so much on Sunday because the weather was bad. | |
| **5.** | ...talked with a friend before going to sleep. | |
| **6.** | ...went to bed around ten o'clock. | |
| **7.** | ...didn't do much on Sunday because they were busy. | |
| **8.** | ...went to the cinema to see a new film. | |
| **9.** | ...mentioned what they did on Saturday. | |
| **10.** | ...listened to some music. | |
| **11.** | ...did many things or went to many places with their friends. | |
| **12.** | ...went to the shopping mall to go window shopping. | |
| **13.** | ...says that last weekend was quite entertaining. | |

# UNIT 7 – ORAL PING-PONG – Person A

| ENGLISH | SPANISH | ENGLISH | SPANISH |
|---|---|---|---|
| **We went to the cinema to see an action film.** | Fuimos al cine para ver una película de acción. | **On Saturday, I didn't do much because I was tired.** | El sábado no hice mucho porque estaba cansado. |
| **On Saturday, I spent a while listening to music alone.** | | **Before going to sleep, I spoke with my friend.** | |
| **On Sunday, I didn't do much because the weather was bad.** | El domingo no hice mucho porque hacía mal tiempo. | **On Friday, I spent a while playing the guitar.** | El viernes pasé un rato tocando la guitarra. |
| **Before going to sleep, I read a book.** | | **My friends and I did many things.** | |
| **Last weekend was very entertaining.** | El fin de semana pasado fue muy entretenido. | **What did you do before going to sleep?** | ¿Qué hiciste antes de dormir? |
| **On Friday, I went to the shopping mall to go window shopping.** | | **Finally, I went to bed at 10:00.** | |
| **My friends and I went to many places.** | Mis amigos y yo fuimos a muchos sitios. | **And later, I spent an hour studying Spanish.** | Y luego pasé una hora estudiando español. |
| **Finally, I went to bed around 9:00.** | | **On Sunday, I didn't do so much because I was busy.** | |
| **For example, I went to the city centre to go for a walk.** | Por ejemplo, fui al centro de la ciudad para dar un paseo. | **On Sunday, I went to the cinema to see a new film.** | El domingo fui al cine para ver una película nueva. |
| **What did you do last weekend?** | | **Last weekend was quite fun.** | |

# UNIT 7 – ORAL PING-PONG – Person B

| ENGLISH | SPANISH | ENGLISH | SPANISH |
|---|---|---|---|
| We went to the cinema to see an action film. | | On Saturday, I didn't do much because I was tired. | |
| On Saturday, I spent a while listening to music alone. | El sábado pasé un rato escuchando música solo. | Before going to sleep, I spoke with my friend. | Antes de dormir hablé con mi amigo. |
| On Sunday, I didn't do much because the weather was bad. | | On Friday, I spent a while playing the guitar. | |
| Before going to sleep, I read a book. | Antes de dormir leí un libro. | My friends and I did many things. | Mis amigos y yo hicimos muchas cosas. |
| Last weekend was very entertaining. | | What did you do before going to sleep? | |
| On Friday, I went to the shopping mall to go window shopping. | El viernes fui al centro comercial para mirar escaparates. | Finally, I went to bed at 10:00. | Finalmente me acosté a las diez. |
| My friends and I went to many places. | | And later, I spent an hour studying Spanish. | |
| Finally, I went to bed around 9:00. | Finalmente me acosté a eso de las nueve. | On Sunday, I didn't do so much because I was busy. | El domingo no hice tanto porque estaba ocupado. |
| For example, I went to the city centre to go for a walk. | | On Sunday, I went to the cinema to see a new film. | |
| What did you do last weekend? | ¿Qué hiciste el fin de semana pasado? | Last weekend was quite fun. | El fin de semana pasado fue bastante divertido. |

# No Snakes No Ladders

**7** — Last weekend was very entertaining.

**8** — On Friday, we went to the city centre to go for a walk.

**23** — I spent a while playing the guitar alone (f) in my house.

**24** — My friends and I went to the cinema to see a new film.

**6** — What did you do on Saturday?

**9** — On Sunday, I didn't do anything because I had a lot of homework.

**22** — Last weekend was quite fun.

**25** — On Friday, I spent an hour searching for information.

**5** — I spent an hour using my phone with my friend (m) at my house.

**10** — And later, I went to the cinema to see a new film.

**21** — What did you do on Sunday?

**26** — On Sunday, I didn't do much because I was busy (f).

**4** — For example, I went to the shopping mall to go window shopping.

**11** — Finally, I went to bed at about 10:00.

**20** — On Sunday, the weather was bad.

**27** — Finally, I went to bed and before going to sleep, I spoke with my friend (m).

**3** — On Saturday, I spent a while studying Spanish.

**12** — What did you do last weekend?

**19** — My friends and I went to the shopping mall.

**28** — I went to the shopping mall and it was quite entertaining.

**2** — And later, I went to the cinema to see a science fiction film.

**13** — Before going to sleep, I listened to a bit of music.

**18** — Last weekend, we went to the city centre.

**29** — What did you do before going to sleep?

**1** — My friends and I went to many places.

**14** — For example, I spent a while searching for information in my bedroom.

**17** — And later, before going to sleep, I read my book.

**30** — I went to the shopping mall and then, I went to the cinema with my friend (m).

**START**

**15** — Finally, I went to bed at 9:00.

**16** — On Saturday, I didn't do anything because I was tired (f).

**FINISH**

# No Snakes No Ladders

**1** — Mis amigos y yo fuimos a muchos sitios.

**2** — Y luego fui al cine para ver una película de ciencia ficción.

**3** — El sábado pasé un rato estudiando español.

**4** — Por ejemplo, fui al centro comercial para mirar escaparates.

**5** — Pasé una hora usando el móvil con mi amigo en mi casa.

**6** — ¿Qué hiciste el sábado?

**7** — El fin de semana pasado fue muy entretenido.

**8** — El viernes fuimos al centro de la ciudad para dar un paseo.

**9** — El domingo no hice nada porque tenía muchos deberes.

**10** — Y luego fui al cine para ver una película nueva.

**11** — Finalmente me acosté a eso de las diez.

**12** — ¿Qué hiciste el fin de semana pasado?

**13** — Antes de dormir escuché un poco de música.

**14** — Por ejemplo, pasé un rato buscando información en mi dormitorio.

**15** — Finalmente me acosté a las nueve.

**SALIDA**

**16** — El sábado no hice nada porque estaba cansada.

**17** — Y luego, antes de dormir leí mi libro.

**18** — El fin de semana pasado fuimos al centro de la ciudad.

**19** — Mis amigos y yo fuimos al centro comercial.

**20** — El domingo hacía mal tiempo.

**21** — ¿Qué hiciste el domingo?

**22** — El fin de semana pasado fue bastante divertido.

**23** — Pasé un rato tocando la guitarra sola en mi casa.

**24** — Mis amigos y yo fuimos al cine para ver una película nueva.

**25** — El viernes pasé una hora buscando información.

**26** — El domingo no hice mucho porque estaba ocupada.

**27** — Finalmente me acosté y antes de dormir hablé con mi amigo.

**28** — Fui al centro comercial y fue bastante entretenido.

**29** — ¿Qué hiciste antes de dormir?

**30** — Fui al centro comercial y luego fui al cine con mi amigo.

**LLEGADA**

# UNIT 7 – STAIRCASE TRANSLATION

Last weekend was very fun. My friends and I did lots of things.

Last weekend was very fun. My friends and I did lots of things. For example, we went to the shopping mall to go window shopping.

Last weekend was very fun. My friends and I did lots of things. For example, we went to the shopping mall to go window shopping. And later, we went to the cinema to see an action film.

Last weekend was very fun. My friends and I did lots of things. For example, we went to the shopping mall to go window shopping. And later, we went to the cinema to see an action film. On Saturday, I spent a while listening to music...

Last weekend was very fun. My friends and I did lots of things. For example, we went to the shopping mall to go window shopping. And later, we went to the cinema to see an action film. On Saturday, I spent a while listening to music with my friend in my bedroom.

Last weekend was very fun. My friends and I did lots of things. For example, we went to the shopping mall to go window shopping. And later, we went to the cinema to see an action film. On Saturday, I spent a while listening to music with my friend in my bedroom. On Sunday, I didn't do so much because I was tired.

Translate the last step here:

# UNIT 7 – FASTER!

## Say:

1. I went to the shopping centre to go window shopping.

2. On Saturday, I spent an hour using my phone.

3. On Sunday, I didn't do anything because it was bad weather.

4. On Friday, we went to the city centre to go for a walk.

5. Last weekend was very entertaining.

6. My friends and I did many things.

7. Finally, I went to bed at about 10:00.

8. And later, I went to the cinema to watch a new film.

9. For example, I spent a while studying Spanish in my house.

10. Before going to sleep, I listened to a bit of music.

|   | Time | Mistakes | Referee's name |
|---|------|----------|----------------|
| 1 |      |          |                |
| 2 |      |          |                |
| 3 |      |          |                |
| 4 |      |          |                |

# UNIT 7 – DETECTIVES & INFORMANTS

| DETECTIVES | Spanish | English |
|------------|---------|---------|
| **¿Qué hiciste el fin de semana pasado?** | | |
| **¿Qué hiciste el sábado?** | | |
| **¿Qué hiciste el domingo?** | | |
| **¿Qué hiciste antes de dormir?** | | |
| **¿A qué hora te acostaste?** | | |
| **¿Adónde fuiste el viernes?** | | |
| **¿Cómo fue el fin de semana pasado?** | | |
| **¿Fuiste al cine?** | | |

### INFORMANTS

| | |
|---|---|
| Antes de dormir hablé con mi amiga. | El sábado pasé un rato escuchando música. |
| El domingo no hice nada porque estaba cansado. | Fuimos al cine para ver una película nueva. |
| El viernes fuimos al centro de la ciudad para dar un paseo. | Me acosté a eso de las diez. |
| El fin de semana pasado fue muy divertido. | El fin de semana pasado fui al centro comercial para mirar escaparates. |

# UNIT 7 – COMMUNICATIVE DRILLS

| 1 | 2 | 3 |
|---|---|---|
| **What did you do last weekend?**<br><br>- Last weekend we did a lot of things.<br><br>**What did you do on Saturday?**<br><br>- On Saturday, I spent an hour playing the guitar. | **What did you do before going to sleep?**<br><br>- Before going to sleep, I read my book. I was tired (m).<br><br>**Why?**<br><br>- Because we did a lot of things. We went to many places. | **My friends and I went to the cinema to see an action film.**<br><br>- What did you do on Friday?<br><br>**On Friday, I didn't do so much because I had a lot of homework.**<br><br>- I also had a lot of homework. |

| 4 | 5 | 6 |
|---|---|---|
| **What did you do on Sunday?**<br><br>- On Sunday, I didn't do much because the weather was bad.<br><br>**And Saturday?**<br><br>- On Saturday, I spent a while using my mobile with my friend (m) in my bedroom. | **What did you do before going to sleep?**<br><br>- I went to bed at about 9:00. Before going to sleep I listened to a bit of music. And you?<br><br>**I went to bed at about 10:00 and before going to sleep, I spoke with my friend.** | **On Saturday, I spent an hour looking for information in my house.**<br><br>- Alone?<br><br>**No, with my friend (m). And you? What did you do on Saturday?**<br><br>- On Saturday, I didn't do anything because the weather was bad. |

| 7 | 8 | 9 |
|---|---|---|
| **Did you go to the shopping centre on Saturday?**<br><br>- No, on Saturday I went to the city centre to go window shopping.<br><br>**And later?**<br><br>- Later, I went to the cinema to see an action film. | **Where did you go on Friday?**<br><br>- On Friday, I didn't do much because I was busy (f).<br><br>**What did you do on Saturday?**<br><br>- On Saturday, I spent a while studying Spanish at home. | **On Sunday, I didn't do anything.**<br><br>- Why?<br><br>**Because I was tired (m). And you?**<br><br>- On Sunday, we did many things. We went to the city centre to go for a walk.<br><br>**How interesting!** |

# UNIT 7 – COMMUNICATIVE DRILLS
# REFEREE CARD

| 1 | 2 | 3 |
|---|---|---|
| **¿Qué hiciste el fin de semana pasado?**<br><br>- El fin de semana pasado hicimos muchas cosas.<br><br>**¿Qué hiciste el sábado?**<br><br>- El sábado pasé una hora tocando la guitarra. | **¿Qué hiciste antes de dormir?**<br><br>- Antes dormir leí mi libro. Estaba cansado.<br><br>**¿Por qué?**<br><br>- Porque hicimos muchas cosas. Fuimos a muchos sitios. | **Mis amigos y yo fuimos al cine para ver una película de acción.**<br><br>- ¿Qué hiciste el viernes?<br><br>**El viernes no hice tanto porque tenía muchos deberes.**<br><br>- Yo también tenía muchos deberes. |

| 4 | 5 | 6 |
|---|---|---|
| **¿Qué hiciste el domingo?**<br><br>- El domingo no hice mucho porque hacía mal tiempo.<br><br>**¿Y el sábado?**<br><br>- El sábado pasé un rato usando el móvil con mi amigo en mi dormitorio. | **¿Qué hiciste antes de dormir?**<br><br>- Me acosté a eso de las nueve. Antes de dormir escuché un poco de música. ¿Y tú?<br><br>**Me acosté a eso de las diez y antes de dormir hablé con mi amigo.** | **El sábado pasé una hora buscando información en mi casa.**<br><br>- ¿Solo?<br><br>**No, con mi amigo. ¿Y tú? ¿Qué hiciste el sábado?**<br><br>- El sábado no hice nada porque hacía mal tiempo. |

| 7 | 8 | 9 |
|---|---|---|
| **¿Fuiste al centro comercial el sábado?**<br><br>- No, el sábado fui al centro de la ciudad para mirar escaparates.<br><br>**¿Y luego?**<br><br>- Luego fui al cine para ver una película de acción. | **¿Adónde fuiste el viernes?**<br><br>- El viernes no hice mucho porque estaba ocupada.<br><br>**¿Qué hiciste el sábado?**<br><br>- El sábado pasé un rato estudiando español en casa. | **El domingo no hice nada.**<br><br>- ¿Por qué?<br><br>**Porque estaba cansado. ¿Y tú?**<br><br>- El domingo hicimos muchas cosas. Fuimos al centro de la ciudad para dar un paseo.<br><br>**¡Qué interesante!** |

# UNIT 7 – SURVEY

| | ¿Cómo te llamas?<br>*What is your name?* | ¿Qué hiciste el fin de semana pasado?<br>*What did you do last weekend?* | ¿Qué hiciste el sábado?<br>*What did you do on Saturday?* | ¿Qué hiciste el domingo?<br>*What did you do on Sunday?* | ¿Qué hiciste antes de dormir?<br>*What did you do before going to sleep?* | ¿A qué hora te acostaste?<br>*What time did you go to bed?* |
|---|---|---|---|---|---|---|
| *e.g.* | Me llamo Juan. | El fin de semana pasado fuimos a muchos sitios. | El sábado pasé una hora usando el móvil. | El domingo no hice nada porque hacía mal tiempo. | Antes de dormir leí mi libro. | Me acosté a eso de las once. |
| 1. | | | | | | |
| 2. | | | | | | |
| 3. | | | | | | |
| 4. | | | | | | |
| 5. | | | | | | |
| 6. | | | | | | |
| 7. | | | | | | |

# UNIT 7 – ANSWERS

## FIND SOMEONE WHO

| | Find someone who... | Name(s) |
|---|---|---|
| **1.** | ...spent some time using their phone alone in their bedroom. | **Conchita** |
| **2.** | ...spent some time playing the guitar at home. | **Nancy** |
| **3.** | ...went to the city centre to go for a walk on Friday. | **Rocío** |
| **4.** | ...didn't do so much on Sunday because the weather was bad. | **Mike** |
| **5.** | ...talked with a friend before going to sleep. | **Isa** |
| **6.** | ...went to bed around ten o'clock. | **Rafael** |
| **7.** | ...didn't do much on Sunday because they were busy. | **Helga** |
| **8.** | ...went to the cinema to see a new film. | **Álvaro/ Manolo** |
| **9.** | ...mentioned what they did on Saturday. | **Jordi/Cesc** |
| **10.** | ...listened to some music. | **Cesc/Yamal** |
| **11.** | ...did many things or went to many places with their friends. | **Jorge/Ángel** |
| **12.** | ...went to the shopping mall to go window shopping. | **Jill** |
| **13.** | ...says that last weekend was quite entertaining. | **Paquito** |

## STAIRCASE TRANSLATION

El fin de semana pasado fue muy divertido. Mis amigos y yo hicimos muchas cosas. Por ejemplo, fuimos al centro comercial para mirar escaparates. Y luego fuimos al cine para ver una película de acción. El sábado pasé un rato escuchando música con mi amigo en mi dormitorio. El domingo no hice tanto porque estaba cansado.

## FASTER!

**REFEREE SOLUTION:**

1. Fui al centro comercial para mirar escaparates.
2. El sábado pasé una hora usando el móvil.
3. El domingo no hice nada porque hacía mal tiempo.
4. El viernes fuimos al centro de la ciudad para dar un paseo.
5. El fin de semana pasado fue muy entretenido.
6. Mis amigos y yo hicimos muchas cosas.
7. Finalmente me acosté a eso de las diez.
8. Y luego fui al cine para ver una película nueva.
9. Por ejemplo, pasé un rato estudiando español en mi casa.
10. Antes de dormir escuché un poco de música.

## DETECTIVES & INFORMANTS

| DETECTIVES | Spanish | English |
|---|---|---|
| **¿Qué hiciste el fin de semana pasado?** | Fui al centro comercial para mirar escaparates. | I went to the shopping mall to go window shopping. |
| **¿Qué hiciste el sábado?** | Pasé un rato escuchando música. | I spent a while listening to music. |
| **¿Qué hiciste el domingo?** | No hice nada porque estaba cansado. | I didn't do anything because I was tired. |
| **¿Qué hiciste antes de dormir?** | Hablé con mi amiga. | I spoke with my friend. |
| **¿A qué hora te acostaste?** | Me acosté a eso de las diez. | I went to bed at about ten. |
| **¿Adónde fuiste el viernes?** | Fuimos al centro de la ciudad para dar un paseo. | We went to the city centre to go for a walk. |
| **¿Cómo fue el fin de semana pasado?** | Fue muy divertido. | It was very fun. |
| **¿Fuiste al cine?** | Fuimos al cine para ver una película nueva. | We went to the cinema to watch a new film. |

# UNIT 8.
## Talking about a recent outing to the cinema with friends

| ¿Cuándo fue la última vez que fuiste al cine? | *When was the last time you went to the cinema?* |
|---|---|
| ¿Qué película viste? | *What film did you watch?* |
| ¿De qué trataba la historia? | *What was the story about?* |
| ¿Te gustó la película? ¿Por qué? | *Did you like the film? Why* |

| **El fin de semana pasado** *Last weekend* | **fui al cine** *I went to the cinema* | **con** | **mis amigos** *my friends* **mi novio/a** *my boyfriend/girlfriend* |
|---|---|---|---|

| **para ver una película** *to see/watch a … film* | **de acción** *action* **de amor** *love* **de animación** *animated* **de aventuras** *adventure* | **de ciencia ficción** *science fiction* **de guerra** *war* **de terror** *horror* |
|---|---|---|

| **La entrada costó cinco euros** *The ticket cost 5 euros* | **Quedamos enfrente del cine** *We met up opposite the cinema* |
|---|---|

| **La historia /película trataba** *The story/film was about* | **de una batalla entre el bien y el mal** *a battle between good and evil* **de la amistad entre un niño y su mascota** *the friendship between a boy and his pet* **de una historia de espionaje** *a spy story* **de una relación de amor** *a love story* **de superhéroes que salvan el mundo** *superheroes who save the world* **del tema del acoso/racismo** *(the theme of) bullying/racism* |
|---|---|

| **Durante la película** *During the film* | **comí** *I ate* | **caramelos** *sweets* **palomitas** *popcorn* **un perrito caliente** *a hot dog* | **y** | **bebí** *I drank* | **Coca-Cola** **limonada** |
|---|---|---|---|---|---|

| **Lo que más me gustó** *What I liked the most* | **fue** *was* | **como termina la historia** *how the story ends* **el actor / la actriz principal** *the main actor/actress* **la banda sonora** *the soundtrack* **la trama** *the plot* |
|---|---|---|
| | **fueron** *were* | **los diálogos** *the dialogues* **los efectos especiales** *the special effects* **las escenas de acción/lucha** *the action/fight scenes* |

| **La actuación de** *The acting by* | **Alba Flores** **Álvaro Morte** | **fue** | **conmovedora** *moving* **impactante** *impactful* **inolvidable** *unforgettable* |
|---|---|---|---|

"

# UNIT 8 – FIND SOMEONE WHO – Student Cards

| | | | |
|---|---|---|---|
| Durante la película comí palomitas y bebí limonada.<br><br>**JUANA** | Lo que más me gustó fue la banda sonora.<br><br>**FEDERICO** | La historia trataba de una relación de amor.<br><br>**ÚRSULA** | La historia trataba del tema del racismo.<br><br>**MACY** |
| Quedamos enfrente del cine.<br><br>**TOBY** | Fui al cine para ver una película de aventuras.<br><br>**DANIELA** | Fui con mi novio para ver una película de animación.<br><br>**REBECCA** | Lo que más me gustó fueron los efectos especiales.<br><br>**ALEJANDRO** |
| La actuación de Alba Flores fue impactante.<br><br>**QUINO** | Durante la película comí caramelos.<br><br>**FILIPPO** | La historia trataba de superhéroes que salvan el mundo.<br><br>**CLAUDIA** | El fin de semana pasado fui al cine con mis amigos.<br><br>**LUCAS** |
| Durante la película bebí Coca-Cola y limonada.<br><br>**JORGE** | Lo que más me gustó fue la banda sonora.<br><br>**SIMON** | La entrada costó cinco euros.<br><br>**RYAN** | Fui con mi novio para ver una película de terror.<br><br>**MARÍA** |

# UNIT 8 – FIND SOMEONE WHO – Student Grid

| ¿Cuándo fue la última vez que fuiste al cine? | *When was the last time you went to the cinema?* |
|---|---|
| ¿Qué película viste? | *What film did you watch?* |
| ¿De qué trataba la historia? | *What was the story about?* |
| ¿Te gustó la película? ¿Por qué? | *Did you like the film? Why?* |

| | Find someone who... | Name(s) |
|---|---|---|
| 1. | ...liked the special effects the most. | |
| 2. | ...went to see an adventure film. | |
| 3. | ...thought Alba Flores' acting was impactful. | |
| 4. | ...said the story was about a love story. | |
| 5. | ...ate sweets during the film or mentions the ticket price. | |
| 6. | ...went with their boyfriend to see an animated film. | |
| 7. | ...said the story was about the theme of racism. | |
| 8. | ...liked the soundtrack the most. | |
| 9. | ...went to the cinema with friends last weekend. | |
| 10. | ...drank lemonade during the film. | |
| 11. | ...met up opposite the cinema. | |
| 12. | ...said the story was about superheroes saving the world. | |
| 13. | ...saw a horror movie with her boyfriend. | |

# UNIT 8 – ORAL PING-PONG – Person A

| ENGLISH | SPANISH | ENGLISH | SPANISH |
|---|---|---|---|
| Last weekend, I went to the cinema with my boyfriend. | El fin de semana pasado fui al cine con mi novio. | I went to the cinema with my girlfriend to see a film. | Fui al cine con mi novia para ver una película. |
| The ticket cost ten euros. | | During the film, I ate popcorn and drank lemonade. | |
| The story was about a battle between good and evil. | La historia trataba de una batalla entre el bien y el mal. | Last weekend, I went to see a love film. | El fin de semana pasado fui a ver una película de amor. |
| We met up opposite the cinema. | | The story was about the friendship between a boy and his pet. | |
| During the film I ate a hot dog. | Durante la película comí un perrito caliente. | What film did you watch? | ¿Qué película viste? |
| What I liked the most were the fight scenes. | | What I liked the most was how the story ends. | |
| The acting by Álvaro Morte was unforgettable. | La actuación de Álvaro Morte fue inolvidable. | The ticket cost eight euros. | La entrada costó ocho euros. |
| ...to see a war film. | | What was the story about? | |
| What I liked the most was the main actor. | Lo que más me gustó fue el actor principal. | What I liked the most were the dialogues. | Lo que más me gustó fueron los diálogos. |
| The story was about the theme of bullying. | | The film was about a spy story. | |

# UNIT 8 – ORAL PING-PONG – Person B

| ENGLISH | SPANISH | ENGLISH | SPANISH |
|---|---|---|---|
| Last weekend, I went to the cinema with my boyfriend. | | I went to the cinema with my girlfriend to see a film. | |
| The ticket cost ten euros. | La entrada costó diez euros. | During the film, I ate popcorn and drank lemonade. | Durante la película comí palomitas y bebí limonada. |
| The story was about a battle between good and evil. | | Last weekend, I went to see a love film. | |
| We met up opposite the cinema. | Quedamos enfrente del cine. | The story was about the friendship between a boy and his pet. | La historia trataba de la amistad entre un niño y su mascota. |
| During the film I ate a hot dog. | | What film did you watch? | |
| What I liked the most were the fight scenes. | Lo que más me gustó fueron las escenas de lucha. | What I liked the most was how the story ends. | Lo que más me gustó fue como termina la historia. |
| The acting by Álvaro Morte was unforgettable. | | The ticket cost eight euros. | |
| ...to see a war film. | ...para ver una película de guerra. | What was the story about? | ¿De qué trataba la historia? |
| What I liked the most was the main actor. | | What I liked the most were the dialogues. | |
| The story was about the theme of bullying. | La historia trataba del tema del acoso. | The film was about a spy story. | La película trataba de una historia de espionaje. |

# No Snakes No Ladders

| | | | | | |
|---|---|---|---|---|---|
| **7** ...to see an action film. | **6** During the film, I ate a hot dog. | **5** Last weekend, I went to the cinema with my girlfriend. | **4** Did you like the film? | **3** The ticket cost nine euros. | **2** What I liked the most was the plot. |
| **8** What was the story about? | **9** The acting by Alba Flores was moving. | **10** The story was about a the theme of bullying. | **11** I went to the cinema with my friends to see an action film. | **12** During the film, I drank Coca-Cola. | **13** What I liked the most were the action scenes. |
| **23** Last weekend, I went to the cinema with my friends. | **22** The story was about superheroes who save the world. | **21** ...to see a science fiction film. | **20** We met up opposite the cinema. | **19** What I liked the most was the soundtrack. | **18** Last weekend, I went to the cinema and drank lemonade. |
| **24** During the love film, I ate popcorn. | **25** What film did you watch? | **26** The acting by Cillian Murphy was impactful. | **27** What I liked the most were the special effects. | **28** When did you go to the cinema? | **29** The story was about the friendship between a boy and his pet. |

**1** The film was about a love story.

**14** The ticket cost 3 euros.

**17** During the film, I ate sweets with my boyfriend.

**30** I went to the cinema with my friends to see a horror film.

**15** When was the last time you went to the cinema?

START

**16** ...to see a film about the theme of racism.

FINISH

# No Snakes No Ladders

| | | | |
|---|---|---|---|
| **7** ...para ver una película de acción. | **6** Durante la película comí un perrito caliente. | **5** El fin de semana pasado fui al cine con mi novia. | **4** ¿Te gustó la película? |
| **8** ¿De qué trataba la historia? | **9** La actuación de Alba Flores fue conmovedora. | **10** La historia trataba del tema del acoso. | **11** Fui al cine con mis amigos para ver una película de acción. |
| **23** El fin de semana pasado fui al cine con mis amigos. | **22** La historia trataba de superhéroes que salvan el mundo. | **21** ...para ver una película de ciencia ficción. | **20** Quedamos enfrente del cine. |
| **24** Durante la película de amor comí palomitas. | **25** ¿Qué película viste? | **26** La actuación de Cillian Murphy fue impactante. | **27** Lo que más me gustó fueron los efectos especiales. |

| | | | |
|---|---|---|---|
| **3** La entrada costó nueve euros. | **2** Lo que más me gustó fue la trama. | **1** La película trataba de una relación de amor. | **SALIDA** |
| **12** Durante la película bebí Coca-Cola. | **13** Lo que más me gustó fueron las escenas de acción. | **14** La entrada costó tres euros. | **15** ¿Cuándo fue la última vez que fuiste al cine? |
| **19** Lo que más me gustó fue la banda sonora. | **18** El fin de semana pasado fui al cine y bebí limonada. | **17** Durante la película comí caramelos con mi novio. | **16** ...para ver una película del tema del racismo. |
| **28** ¿Cuándo fuiste al cine? | **29** La historia trataba de la amistad entre un niño y su mascota. | **30** Fui al cine con mis amigos para ver una película de terror. | **LLEGADA** |

# UNIT 8 – STAIRCASE TRANSLATION

Last weekend, I went to the cinema with my friends...

Last weekend, I went to the cinema with my friends to see an adventure film. The ticket cost 4 euros.

Last weekend, I went to the cinema with my friends to see an adventure film. The ticket cost 4 euros. We met up opposite the cinema. The story was about superheroes who save the world.

Last weekend, I went to the cinema with my friends to see an adventure film. The ticket cost 4 euros. We met up opposite the cinema. The story was about superheroes who save the world. During the film, I ate popcorn and drank Coca-Cola.

Last weekend, I went to the cinema with my friends to see an adventure film. The ticket cost 4 euros. We met up opposite the cinema. The story was about superheroes who save the world. During the film, I ate popcorn and drank Coca-Cola. What I liked the most was the main actor.

Last weekend, I went to the cinema with my friends to see an adventure film. The ticket cost 4 euros. We met up opposite the cinema. The story was about superheroes who save the world. During the film, I ate popcorn and drank Coca-Cola. What I liked the most was the main actor. The acting by Samuel L. Jackson was unforgettable.

Translate the last step here:

# ⏱ UNIT 8 – FASTER! 🚀

## Say:

1. Last weekend, I went to the cinema with my boyfriend.

2. The ticket cost 10 euros.

3. The story was about a battle between good and evil.

4. What film did you watch?

5. I went to the cinema to see a war film.

6. During the film, I ate a hot dog and drank Coca-Cola.

7. Did you like the film?

8. What I liked the most was the plot.

9. The acting by Bad Bunny was unforgettable.

10. When was the last time you went to the cinema?

|   | Time | Mistakes | Referee's name |
|---|---|---|---|
| 1 |   |   |   |
| 2 |   |   |   |
| 3 |   |   |   |
| 4 |   |   |   |

 # UNIT 8 – FAST & FURIOUS 
### Focus on film genres

1. Fui al cine para ver una película de ____________.  *love*

2. El sábado pasado fui con mi novia para ver una película de __________.  *action*

3. La película trataba de ____ ____________ _____ ______________.  *a spy story*

4. Durante la película de ________________ comí caramelos.  *animated*

5. Fui con mi novio para ver una película de __________________.  *war*

6. Me gustó la película de ______________.  *adventure*

7. La historia trataba del _______ _____ __________.  *the theme of bullying*

8. La actuación en la película de _________ __________ fue inolvidable.  *science fiction*

9. La entrada a la película de __________ costó ocho euros.  *horror*

10. No me gustó la ____________ ___ _________.  *love story*

|   | Time 1 | Time 2 | Time 3 | Time 4 |
|---|---|---|---|---|
| Time |   |   |   |   |
| Mistakes |   |   |   |   |

# UNIT 8 – COMMUNICATIVE DRILLS

| 1 | 2 | 3 |
|---|---|---|
| **When was the last time you went to the cinema?**<br><br>- Last weekend, I went to the cinema with my girlfriend.<br><br>**What film did you watch?**<br><br>- An adventure film and it was about superheroes who save the world. | **Did you like the film?**<br><br>- Yes, a lot.<br><br>**Why did you like it?**<br><br>- Because the acting by Al Pacino was unforgettable. And I ate popcorn!<br><br>**Very good!** | **Last weekend, I went with my friends to see a horror film.**<br><br>- What was the story about?<br><br>**The story was about a battle between good and evil.**<br><br>- Did you like the film?<br><br>**No, I didn't like it.** |
| **4** | **5** | **6** |
| **What film did you watch?**<br><br>- I went to the cinema with my boyfriend to see a love film.<br><br>**Did you like the film?**<br><br>- What I liked the most was the plot. During the film, I ate sweets and drank Coca-Cola. | **Why did you like the film?**<br><br>- What I liked the most were the special effects. The ticket cost six euros.<br><br>**What film did you watch?**<br><br>- The film was about a spy story. | **When was the last time you went to the cinema?**<br><br>- Last weekend.<br><br>**Did you go with your girlfriend?**<br><br>- No, I went with my friends. We met opposite the cinema. |
| **7** | **8** | **9** |
| **During the film, I ate a hot dog and I drank lemonade.**<br><br>- Did you like the film?<br><br>**Yes. I liked it. I liked the acting by Kate Winslet.**<br><br>- Yes it was moving. | **Last weekend, I went to the cinema with my girlfriend to watch a science fiction film. And you?**<br><br>- I went to the cinema with my friend to watch a war film. The ticket cost 20 euros! | **What film did you watch last weekend?**<br><br>- I went with my friends to see an animated film. And you?<br><br>**I went to see a film that was about the theme of racism.** |

# UNIT 8 – COMMUNICATIVE DRILLS
## REFEREE CARD

| 1 | 2 | 3 |
|---|---|---|
| **¿Cuándo fue la última vez que fuiste al cine?**<br><br>- El fin de semana pasado fui al cine con mi novia.<br><br>**¿Qué película viste?**<br><br>- Una película de aventuras y trataba de superhéroes que salvan el mundo. | **¿Te gustó la película?**<br><br>- Sí, mucho.<br><br>**¿Por qué te gustó?**<br><br>- Porque la actuación de Al Pacino fue inolvidable. ¡Y comí palomitas!<br><br>**¡Muy bien!** | **El fin de semana pasado fui con mis amigos para ver una película de terror.**<br><br>- ¿De qué trataba la historia?<br><br>**La historia trataba de una batalla entre bien y mal.**<br><br>- ¿Te gustó la película?<br><br>**No, no me gustó.** |
| **4** | **5** | **6** |
| **¿Qué película viste?**<br><br>- Fui al cine con mi novio para ver una película de amor.<br><br>**¿Te gustó la película?**<br><br>- Lo que más me gustó fue la trama. Durante la película comí caramelos y bebí Coca-Cola. | **¿Por qué te gustó la película?**<br><br>- Lo que más me gustó fueron los efectos especiales. La entrada costó seis euros.<br><br>**¿Qué película viste?**<br><br>- La película trataba de una historia de espionaje. | **¿Cuándo fue la última vez que fuiste al cine?**<br><br>- El fin de semana pasado.<br><br>**¿Fuiste con tu novia?**<br><br>- No, fui con mis amigos. Quedamos enfrente del cine. |
| **7** | **8** | **9** |
| **Durante la película comí un perrito caliente y bebí limonada.**<br><br>- ¿Te gustó la película?<br><br>**Sí. Me gustó. Me gustó la actuación de Kate Winslet.**<br><br>- Sí, fue conmovedora. | **El fin de semana pasado fui al cine con mi novia para ver una película de ciencia ficción. ¿Y tú?**<br><br>- Fui al cine con mi amigo para ver una película de guerra. ¡La entrada costó veinte euros! | **¿Qué película viste el fin de semana pasado?**<br><br>- Fui con mis amigos para ver una película de animación. ¿Y tú?<br><br>**Fui para ver una película que trataba del tema del racismo.** |

# UNIT 8 – SURVEY

| | ¿Cómo te llamas?<br>*What is your name?* | ¿Cuándo fue la última vez que fuiste al cine?<br>*When was the last time that you went to the cinema?* | ¿Qué película viste?<br>*What film did you watch?* | ¿De qué trataba la historia?<br>*What was the story about?* | ¿Te gustó la película?<br>*Did you like the film?* | ¿Qué hiciste durante la película?<br>*What did you do during the film?* |
|---|---|---|---|---|---|---|
| *e.g.* | *Me llamo Juan.* | *El fin de semana pasado fui al cine con mi novia.* | *Vi una película de amor.* | *La historia trataba de una relación de amor.* | *Sí. Lo que más me gustó fue la trama.* | *Durante la película comí caramelos.* |
| 1. | | | | | | |
| 2. | | | | | | |
| 3. | | | | | | |
| 4. | | | | | | |
| 5. | | | | | | |
| 6. | | | | | | |
| 7. | | | | | | |

# UNIT 8 – ANSWERS

## FIND SOMEONE WHO

| Find someone who/whose... | | Name(s) |
|---|---|---|
| **1.** | ...liked the special effects the most. | **Alejandro** |
| **2.** | ...went to see an adventure film. | **Daniela** |
| **3.** | ...thought Alba Flores' acting was impactful. | **Quino** |
| **4.** | ...said the story was about a love story. | **Úrsula** |
| **5.** | ...ate sweets during the film or mentions the ticket price. | **Filippo/Ryan** |
| **6.** | ...went with their boyfriend to see an animated film. | **Rebecca** |
| **7.** | ...said the story was about the theme of racism. | **Macy** |
| **8.** | ...liked the soundtrack the most. | **Simon/Federico** |
| **9.** | ...went to the cinema with friends last weekend. | **Lucas** |
| **10.** | ...drank lemonade during the film. | **Juana/Jorge** |
| **11.** | ...met up opposite the cinema. | **Toby** |
| **12.** | ...said the story was about superheroes saving the world. | **Claudia** |
| **13.** | ...saw a horror movie with her boyfriend. | **María** |

## STAIRCASE TRANSLATION

El fin de semana pasado fui al cine con mis amigos para ver una película de aventuras. La entrada costó cuatro euros. Quedamos enfrente del cine. La historia trataba de superhéroes que salvan el mundo. Durante la película comí palomitas y bebí Coca-Cola. Lo que más me gustó fue el actor principal. La actuación de Samuel L. Jackson fue inolvidable.

## FASTER!

**REFEREE SOLUTION:**

1. El fin de semana pasado fui al cine con mi novio.
2. La entrada costó 10 euros.
3. La historia trataba de una batalla entre el bien y el mal.
4. ¿Qué película viste?
5. Fui al cine para ver una película de guerra.
6. Durante la película comí un perrito caliente y bebí Coca-Cola.
7. ¿Te gustó la película?
8. Lo que más me gustó fue la trama.
9. La actuación de Bad Bunny fue inolvidable.
10. ¿Cuándo fue la última vez que fuiste al cine?

## FAST & FURIOUS

1. Fui al cine para ver una película de **amor**.
2. El sábado pasado fui con mi novia para ver una película de **acción**.
3. La película trataba de **una historia de espionaje**.
4. Durante la película de **animación** comí caramelos.
5. Fui con mi novio para ver una película de **guerra**.
6. Me gustó la película de **aventuras**.
7. La historia trataba del **tema del acoso**.
8. La actuación en la película de **ciencia ficción** fue inolvidable.
9. La entrada a la película de **terror** costó ocho euros.
10. No me gustó la **relación de amor**.

# UNIT 9.
## Talking about a birthday party we went to

| ¿Dónde fue la fiesta de tu amigo/a? | Where was your friend's party? |
|---|---|
| ¿Qué hiciste durante la fiesta? | What did you do during the party? |
| ¿Qué le regalaste a tu amigo/a? | What (gift) did you give your friend? |

| El fin de semana pasado | fue la fiesta de cumpleaños | de mi amigo/a |
|---|---|---|
| *Last weekend* | *was the birthday party* | *of my friend* |

| Mi amigo/a | hizo la fiesta | en un centro comercial | *in a shopping mall* |
|---|---|---|---|
| | *had the party* | en un parque de atracciones | *at a theme park* |
| | | en un restaurante | *at a restaurant* |
| | | en su casa | *at their house* |

**Había mucha comida y bebida**     *There was a lot of food and drink*

| comí | *I ate* | comida rápida | *fast food* | patatas fritas | *French fries* |
|---|---|---|---|---|---|
| comimos | *we ate* | pastel | *cake* | pizza | |
| bebí | *I drank* | Coca-Cola | | refrescos | *soft drinks* |
| bebimos | *we drank* | limonada | *lemonade* | zumo de naranja | *orange juice* |

**Durante la fiesta**     *During the party*

| | | bailando | *dancing* |
|---|---|---|---|
| Nos divertimos | | cantando karaoke | *singing karaoke* |
| *We had fun* | | contando chistes | *telling jokes* |
| | | escuchando música | *listening to music* |
| Pasamos una hora / dos horas | | sacando fotos | *taking photos* |
| *We spent one/two hours* | | jugando a juegos | *playing games* |
| | | viendo una película | *watching a film* |

| Le di un regalo | barato | *cheap* | a mi amigo/a |
|---|---|---|---|
| *I gave a … gift* | caro | *expensive* | *to my friend* |
| | chulo | *cool* | |
| | original | *original* | |

| Le compré | una camiseta | *a t-shirt* | |
|---|---|---|---|
| *I bought* | un collar | *a necklace* | y le gustó mucho |
| Le regalé | un reloj | *a watch* | *and he/she liked it a lot* |
| *I gave (gifted)* | una pulsera | *a bracelet* | |
| | una tarjeta de regalo | *a gift card* | |

| La fiesta fue | la leche | *awesome (the milk)* | Me lo pasé genial |
|---|---|---|---|
| *The party was* | muy divertida | *very fun* | *I had a great time* |

# UNIT 9 – FIND SOMEONE WHO – Student Cards

| | | | |
|---|---|---|---|
| Nos divertimos cantando karaoke.<br><br>**FELICIANO** | Le di un regalo chulo a mi amigo.<br><br>**RAÚL** | La fiesta fue muy divertida.<br><br>**ISABELA** | Había mucha comida y bebida.<br><br>**FERNANDO** |
| Mi amigo hizo la fiesta en su casa.<br><br>**CONCHITA** | Comí patatas fritas y bebí refrescos.<br><br>**RAMONA** | Pasamos dos horas escuchando música.<br><br>**BELÉN** | El fin de semana pasado fue la fiesta de cumpleaños de mi amiga.<br>**SIMONA** |
| Pasamos una hora viendo una película.<br><br>**RAFA** | Mi amiga hizo la fiesta en su casa.<br><br>**PAULA** | Nos divertimos jugando a juegos.<br><br>**LAUTARO** | Le compré una pulsera y le gustó mucho.<br><br>**ORIOL** |
| Le regalé un reloj y un collar caro a mi amigo.<br><br>**ALBERTO** | Le di un regalo caro a mi amigo.<br><br>**PATRICIA** | Comimos comida rápida y nos divertimos.<br><br>**ROSA** | Nos divertimos contando chistes.<br><br>**MILLIE** |

# UNIT 9 – FIND SOMEONE WHO – Student Grid

| ¿Dónde fue la fiesta de tu amigo/a? | *Where was your friend's party?* |
|---|---|
| ¿Qué hiciste durante la fiesta? | *What did you do during the party?* |
| ¿Qué le regalaste a tu amigo/a? | *What (gift) did you give your friend?* |

| | Find someone who... | Name(s) |
|---|---|---|
| **1.** | ...had fun singing karaoke. | |
| **2.** | ...said their friend hosted the party at their house. | |
| **3.** | ...spent an hour watching a film. | |
| **4.** | ...gave an expensive gift to their friend. | |
| **5.** | ... played games. | |
| **6.** | ...said there was a lot of food and drink. | |
| **7.** | ...bought a bracelet and their friend liked it a lot. | |
| **8.** | ...said last weekend was their friend's birthday party. | |
| **9.** | ...gave a cool gift to their friend. | |
| **10.** | ...spent two hours listening to music. | |
| **11.** | ...said the party was very fun. | |
| **12.** | ...ate fast food and had fun. | |
| **13** | ...ate French fries and drank soft drinks. | |
| **14** | ...had fun telling jokes. | |

# UNIT 9 – ORAL PING-PONG – Person A

| ENGLISH | SPANISH | ENGLISH | SPANISH |
|---|---|---|---|
| We drank orange juice. | Bebimos zumo de naranja. | I gave my friend an expensive watch. | Le regalé un reloj caro a mi amiga. |
| I gave my friend a cheap gift. | | There was a lot of food and drink. | |
| I gave them a gift card and they liked it. | Le regalé una tarjeta de regalo y le gustó. | During the party, I ate pizza and French fries. | Durante la fiesta comí pizza y patatas fritas. |
| We had fun watching a film. | | I had a great time. | |
| We spent an hour telling jokes. | Pasamos una hora contando chistes. | My friend had the party at a restaurant. | Mi amiga hizo la fiesta en un restaurante. |
| My friend had the party at a theme park. | | What did you do during the party? | |
| Last weekend was my friend's birthday party. | El fin de semana pasado fue la fiesta de cumpleaños de mi amigo. | I bought a necklace and a T-shirt and they liked it. | Le compré un collar y una camiseta y le gustó. |
| I bought them a T-shirt and they liked it a lot. | | During the party, we had fun dancing. | |
| The party was awesome. | La fiesta fue la leche. | What did you give your friend? | ¿Qué le regalaste a tu amigo? |
| Where was your friend's party? | | We had fun telling jokes. | |

# UNIT 9 – ORAL PING-PONG – Person B

| ENGLISH | SPANISH | ENGLISH | SPANISH |
|---|---|---|---|
| artWe drank orange juice. | | I gave my friend an expensive watch. | |
| I gave my friend a cheap gift. | Le di un regalo barato a mi amigo. | There was a lot of food and drink. | Había mucha comida y bebida. |
| I gave them a gift card and they liked it. | | During the party, I ate pizza and French fries. | |
| We had fun watching a film. | Nos divertimos viendo una película. | I had a great time. | Me lo pasé genial. |
| We spent an hour telling jokes. | | My friend had the party at a restaurant. | |
| My friend had the party at a theme park. | Mi amigo hizo la fiesta en un parque de atracciones. | What did you do during the party? | ¿Qué hiciste durante la fiesta? |
| Last weekend was my friend's birthday party. | | I bought a necklace and a T-shirt and they liked it. | |
| I bought them a T-shirt and they liked it a lot. | Le compré una camiseta y le gustó mucho. | During the party, we had fun dancing. | Durante la fiesta nos divertimos bailando. |
| The party was awesome. | | What did you give your friend? | |
| Where was your friend's party? | ¿Dónde fue la fiesta de tu amigo? | We had fun telling jokes. | Nos divertimos contando chistes. |

# No Snakes No Ladders

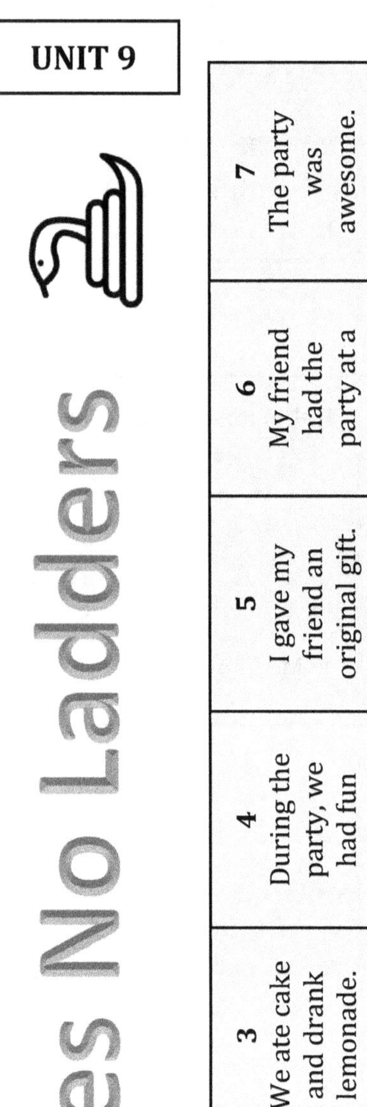

**START**

1. We spent an hour playing games.
2. There was a lot of food and drink.
3. We ate cake and drank lemonade.
4. During the party, we had fun dancing.
5. I gave my friend an original gift.
6. My friend had the party at a restaurant.
7. The party was awesome.
8. Where was your friend's party?
9. I gifted him a gift card.
10. We spent an hour telling jokes.
11. Last weekend was the birthday party of my brother.
12. During the party, I drank Coca-Cola.
13. We had fun watching a film.
14. What did you do during the party?
15. I had a great time.
16. I gifted her a cool necklace and she liked it a lot.
17. I ate fast food at a restaurant.
18. Last weekend my friend had the party at his house.
19. The party was very fun.
20. I gave my friend a cheap but cool gift.
21. During the party, we had fun singing karaoke.
22. What did you give your friend (f)?
23. I drank orange juice at a shopping mall.
24. There was a lot of fast food and soft drinks.
25. I bought her a T-shirt and she didn't like it.
26. We spent three hours at the birthday party.
27. Last weekend, we had fun dancing.
28. During the party, I drank soft drinks.
29. We spent an hour listening to music at a restaurant.
30. I bought him a bracelet and an expensive necklace.

**FINISH**

# No Snakes No Ladders

| | | | |
|---|---|---|---|
| **7** La fiesta fue la leche. | **8** ¿Dónde fue la fiesta de tu amigo? | **23** Bebí zumo de naranja en un centro comercial. | **24** Había mucha comida rápida y refrescos. |
| **6** Mi amigo hizo la fiesta en un restaurante. | **9** Le regalé una tarjeta de regalo. | **22** ¿Qué le regalaste a tu amiga? | **25** Le compré una camiseta y no le gustó. |
| **5** Le di un regalo original a mi amiga. | **10** Pasamos una hora contando chistes. | **21** Durante la fiesta nos divertimos cantando karaoke. | **26** Pasamos tres horas en la fiesta de cumpleaños. |
| **4** Durante la fiesta nos divertimos bailando. | **11** El fin de semana pasado fue la fiesta de cumpleaños de mi hermano. | **20** Le di un regalo barato pero chulo a mi amigo. | **27** El fin de semana pasado nos divertimos bailando. |
| **3** Comimos pastel y bebimos limonada. | **12** Durante la fiesta bebí Coca-Cola. | **19** La fiesta fue muy divertida. | **28** Durante la fiesta bebí refrescos. |
| **2** Había mucha comida y bebida. | **13** Nos divertimos viendo una película. | **18** El fin de semana pasado mi amigo hizo la fiesta en su casa. | **29** Pasamos una hora escuchando música en un restaurante. |
| **1** Pasamos una hora jugando a juegos. | **14** ¿Qué hiciste durante la fiesta? | **17** Comí comida rápida en un restaurante. | **30** Le compré una pulsera y un collar caro. |
| **SALIDA** | **15** Me lo pasé genial. | **16** Le regalé un collar chulo y le gustó mucho. | **LLEGADA** |

# UNIT 9 – STAIRCASE TRANSLATION

Last weekend was the birthday party of my friend.

Last weekend was the birthday party of my friend. My friend had the party at their house.

Last weekend was the birthday party of my friend. My friend had the party at their house. There was a lot of food and drink and I ate fast food.

Last weekend was the birthday party of my friend. My friend had the party at their house. There was a lot of food and drink and I ate fast food. During the party, we spent two hours listening to music and dancing.

Last weekend was the birthday party of my friend. My friend had the party at their house. There was a lot of food and drink and I ate fast food. During the party, we spent two hours listening to music and dancing. I gave a cool gift to my friend. I bought a watch and he liked it a lot.

Last weekend was the birthday party of my friend. My friend had the party at their house. There was a lot of food and drink and I ate fast food. During the party, we spent two hours listening to music and dancing. I gave a cool gift to my friend. I bought a watch and he liked it a lot. The party was very fun.

Translate the last step here:

# UNIT 9 – FASTER!

**Say:**

1. Where was your friend's party?

2. My friend had the party at a theme park.

3. There was lots of food and drink and I ate fast food.

4. What did you do during the party?

5. During the party, we spent two hours listening to music.

6. We had fun singing karaoke and telling jokes.

7. What (gift) did you give your friend?

8. I gave her an expensive gift. I bought a watch and she liked it a lot.

|   | Time | Mistakes | Referee's name |
|---|------|----------|----------------|
| **1** |  |  |  |
| **2** |  |  |  |
| **3** |  |  |  |
| **4** |  |  |  |

# UNIT 9 – THINGS IN COMMON

Write your own answers to the questions then interview three friends and make a note of what things you have in common.

|  | Yo<br>*(Your own answer)* | 1 | 2 | 3 |
|---|---|---|---|---|
| **¿Dónde fue la fiesta de tu amigo/a?** |  |  |  |  |
| **¿Qué hiciste durante la fiesta?** |  |  |  |  |
| **¿Qué comiste?** |  |  |  |  |
| **¿Qué bebiste?** |  |  |  |  |
| **¿Qué le regalaste a tu amigo/a?** |  |  |  |  |
| **¿Le gustó el regalo?** |  |  |  |  |
| **¿Cómo fue la fiesta?** |  |  |  |  |

# UNIT 9 – COMMUNICATIVE DRILLS

| 1 | 2 | 3 |
|---|---|---|
| **Where was your friend's party?**<br><br>- My friend had the party at his house. There was a lot of food.<br><br>**What did you do at the party?**<br><br>- During the party, we spent an hour dancing. | **What did you give your friend?**<br><br>- I gave her a bracelet and she liked it. And you?<br><br>**I gave her a cool necklace. She liked it very much.**<br><br>- How cool! I had a great time. | **Last weekend was my brother's birthday party.**<br><br>- Where was the party?<br><br>**What did you give your brother?**<br><br>- I bought him a cheap T-shirt and he didn't like it. |

| 4 | 5 | 6 |
|---|---|---|
| **What did you do during the party?**<br><br>- During the party, we ate cake and drank soft drinks. And you?<br><br>**I spent an hour playing games.**<br><br>-Me too. We had fun playing games and telling jokes. | **Where was your dad's party?**<br><br>- My dad had the party at a restaurant.<br><br>**What did you give your dad?**<br><br>- I gave him an expensive gift. I bought him an original watch and he liked it very much. | **The party was awesome!**<br><br>-Yes. I had a great time with my friends.<br><br>**What did you do during the party?**<br><br>- During the party, I ate chips and drank Coca-Cola. And you?<br><br>**We had fun watching a film and singing.** |

| 7 | 8 | 9 |
|---|---|---|
| **Hello! How are you?**<br><br>- Very good, thank you. Where was your friend's birthday party (f)?<br><br>**My friend (f) had the party at a shopping mall.**<br><br>- And what did you give her?<br><br>**I gave her a 10 euro gift card.** | **I went to my sister's party. I went with my family.**<br><br>- What did you do during your sister's party?<br><br>**A lot! We had fun dancing, playing games and listening to music.**<br><br>- Did she do the party at her house?<br><br>**No, he had the party in a Spanish restaurant. It was awesome (the milk)!** | **What did you do during your mum's party?**<br><br>- I ate pizza because she had the party at her Italian friend's house.<br><br>**How cool! What did you give your mother?**<br><br>- I bought her a necklace and she liked it very much. The party was fun. |

# UNIT 9 – COMMUNICATIVE DRILLS
## REFEREE CARD

| 1 | 2 | 3 |
|---|---|---|
| **¿Dónde fue la fiesta de tu amigo?**<br><br>- Mi amigo hizo la fiesta en su casa. Había mucha comida.<br><br>**¿Qué hiciste en la fiesta?**<br><br>- Durante la fiesta pasamos una hora bailando. | **¿Qué le regalaste a tu amiga?**<br><br>- Le regalé una pulsera y le gustó. ¿Y tú?<br><br>**Le regalé un collar chulo. Le gustó mucho.**<br><br>- ¡Que chulo! Me lo pasé genial. | **El fin de semana pasado fue la fiesta de cumpleaños de mi hermano.**<br><br>- ¿Dónde fue la fiesta?<br><br>**¿Qué le regalaste a tu hermano?**<br><br>- Le compré una camiseta barata y no le gustó. |
| **4** | **5** | **6** |
| **¿Qué hiciste durante la fiesta?**<br><br>- Durante la fiesta comimos pastel y bebimos refrescos. ¿Y tú?<br><br>**Pasé una hora jugando a juegos.**<br><br>- Yo también. Nos divertimos jugando a juegos y contando chistes. | **¿Dónde fue la fiesta de tu padre?**<br><br>- Mi padre hizo la fiesta en un restaurante.<br><br>**¿Qué le regalaste a tu padre?**<br><br>- Le di un regalo caro. Le compré un reloj original y le gustó mucho. | **¡La fiesta fue la leche!**<br><br>- Sí. Me lo pasé genial con mis amigos.<br><br>**¿Qué hiciste durante la fiesta?**<br><br>- Durante la fiesta comí patatas fritas y bebí Coca-Cola. ¿Y tú?<br><br>**Nos divertimos viendo una película y cantando.** |
| **7** | **8** | **9** |
| **¡Hola! ¿Qué tal?**<br><br>- Muy bien, gracias. ¿Dónde fue la fiesta de cumpleaños de tu amiga?<br><br>**Mi amiga hizo la fiesta en un centro comercial.**<br><br>- ¿Y qué le regalaste?<br><br>**Le regalé una tarjeta de regalo de diez euros.** | **Fui a la fiesta de mi hermana. Fui con mi familia.**<br><br>- ¿Qué hiciste durante la fiesta de tu hermana?<br><br>**¡Mucho! Nos divertimos bailando, jugando a juegos y escuchando música.**<br><br>- ¿Hizo la fiesta en su casa?<br><br>**No, hizo la fiesta en un restaurante español. ¡Fue la leche!** | **¿Qué hiciste durante la fiesta de tu madre?**<br><br>- Comí pizza porque hizo la fiesta en casa de su amiga italiana.<br><br>**¡Qué guay! ¿Qué le regalaste a tu madre?**<br><br>- Le compré un collar y le gustó mucho. La fiesta fue divertida. |

# UNIT 9 – SURVEY

| | ¿Cómo te llamas? *What is your name?* | ¿Dónde fue la fiesta de tu amigo/a? *Where was your friend's party?* | ¿Qué hiciste durante la fiesta? *What did you do during the party?* | ¿Qué comiste y bebiste? *What did you eat and drink?* | ¿Qué le regalaste a tu amigo/a? *What did you give your friend?* | ¿Cómo fue la fiesta? *How was the party?* |
|---|---|---|---|---|---|---|
| *e.g.* | *Me llamo Juan.* | *Mi amiga hizo la fiesta en su casa.* | *Durante la fiesta pasamos dos horas bailando.* | *Comí patatas fritas y bebí limonada.* | *Le regalé una camiseta y le gustó.* | *La fiesta fue muy divertida.* |
| **1.** | | | | | | |
| **2.** | | | | | | |
| **3.** | | | | | | |
| **4.** | | | | | | |
| **5.** | | | | | | |
| **6.** | | | | | | |
| **7.** | | | | | | |

# UNIT 9 – ANSWERS

## FIND SOMEONE WHO

| Find someone who/whose... | | Name(s) |
|---|---|---|
| **1.** | ...had fun singing karaoke. | **Feliciano** |
| **2.** | ...said their friend hosted the party at their house. | **Conchita/Paula** |
| **3.** | ...spent an hour watching a film. | **Rafa** |
| **4.** | ...gave an expensive gift to their friend. | **Patricia/Alberto** |
| **5.** | ...played games. | **Lautaro** |
| **6.** | ...said there was a lot of food and drink. | **Fernando** |
| **7.** | ...bought a bracelet and their friend liked it a lot. | **Oriol** |
| **8.** | ...said last weekend was their friend's birthday party. | **Simona** |
| **9.** | ...gave a cool gift to their friend. | **Raúl** |
| **10.** | ...spent two hours listening to music. | **Belén** |
| **11.** | ...said the party was very fun. | **Isabella** |
| **12.** | ...ate fast food and had fun. | **Rosa** |
| **13** | ...ate French fries and drank soft drinks. | **Ramona** |
| **14** | ...had fun telling jokes. | **Millie** |

## STAIRCASE TRANSLATION

El fin de semana pasado fue la fiesta de cumpleaños de mi amigo. Mi amigo hizo la fiesta en su casa. Había mucha comida y bebida y comí comida rápida. Durante la fiesta pasamos dos horas escuchando música y bailando. Le di un regalo chulo a mi amigo. Le compré un reloj y le gustó mucho. La fiesta fue muy divertida.

## FASTER!

**REFEREE SOLUTION:**

1. ¿Dónde fue la fiesta de tu amigo?
2. Mi amigo hizo la fiesta en un parque temático.
3. Había mucha comida y bebida y comí comida rápida.
4. ¿Qué hiciste durante la fiesta?
5. Durante la fiesta pasamos dos horas escuchando música.
6. Nos divertimos cantando karaoke y contando chistes.
7. ¿Qué regalo le diste a tu amigo?
8. Le di un regalo caro. Le compré un reloj y le gustó mucho.

# UNIT 10.  *OPTIONAL*
## Making plans for next weekend

| ¿Qué vas a hacer el fin de semana que viene? | *What are you going to do next weekend?* |
|---|---|
| ¿Qué planes tienes para el sábado/domingo? | *What plans do you have for Saturday/Sunday?* |
| ¿Qué te gustaría hacer? | *What would you like to do?* |
| ¿Qué tienes que hacer? | *What do you have to do?* |

| | | | hacer muchas cosas | *to do many things* | |
|---|---|---|---|---|---|
| **El fin de semana que viene** *Next weekend* | **me gustaría** *I would like* | **ir** *to go* | al cine | *to the cinema* | |
| | | | al centro comercial | *to the shopping mall* | |
| | | | al estadio | *to the stadium* | |
| | | | al parque | *to the park* | |
| | | | de compras | *shopping* | |
| | | | de paseo | *for a walk* | |
| | | | de pesca | *fishing* | |
| | | pasar tiempo con | *to spend time with* | **mis amigos/as** | |
| | | quedar con | *to meet up with* | **mi familia** | |

| **El sábado** *On Saturday* | **por la mañana** *morning* **por la tarde** *afternoon* | **me gustaría** *I would like* | jugar a la Play | *to play on the PlayStation* |
|---|---|---|---|---|
| | | | salir con mis amigos | *to go out with my friends* |
| | | | tocar el piano | *to play the piano* |

| **Luego** *Later* | **el domingo** *on Sunday* | **voy a** *I'm going to* | escuchar música | *listen to music* |
|---|---|---|---|---|
| | | | hablar con mis amigos | *speak with my friends* |
| | | | jugar a videojuegos | *play video games* |
| | | | leer un libro | *read a book* |
| | | | meterme en internet | *go on the internet* |
| | | | mirar mi Instagram | *look at my Insta* |

| **Sin embargo** *However* | **también tengo que** *I also have to* | estudiar para un examen de *study for a … exam* | **español** **ciencias** **matemáticas** |
|---|---|---|---|
| | | hacer los deberes de *do my … homework* | |
| | | ayudar en casa | *help at home* |
| | | buscar información (para mis deberes) | *look for information (for my HW)* |
| | | sacar al perro | *take out the dog* |

| **Si tengo tiempo** *If I have time* | **me gustaría** *I would like* | **pasar** *to spend* | **una hora** *an hour* **un rato** *a while* | **charlando con mi amigo/a** *chatting to my friend* **entrenando en el gimnasio** *training in the gym* **tocando la guitarra** *playing the guitar* |
|---|---|---|---|---|

| **Pienso que será** *I think it will be* | **divertido** *fun* | **entretenido** *entertaining* | **relajante** *relaxing* |
|---|---|---|---|

# UNIT 10 – FIND SOMEONE WHO – Student Cards

| | | | |
|---|---|---|---|
| El fin de semana que viene me gustaría ir al cine.<br><br>**OLIVIA** | El sábado por la tarde me gustaría tocar el piano.<br><br>**DAVID** | Luego voy a leer un libro.<br><br>**PEPE** | Si tengo tiempo me gustaría pasar una hora tocando la guitarra.<br><br>**WILLIAM** |
| El domingo me gustaría ir de compras.<br><br>**SERGIO** | Luego voy a jugar a videojuegos.<br><br>**PEPITA** | Si tengo tiempo voy a hablar con mis amigos.<br><br>**CARLOS** | El fin de semana que viene me gustaría pasar tiempo con mi familia.<br><br>**DANIELA** |
| Luego me gustaría ir al centro comercial.<br><br>**GABRIELA** | Luego el domingo voy a escuchar música.<br><br>**ESTHER** | También tengo que sacar al perro.<br><br>**CARMEN** | Tengo que estudiar para un examen de ciencias.<br><br>**ANDRÉS** |
| El sábado por la mañana me gustaría salir con mis amigos.<br><br>**VÍCTOR** | El domingo por la tarde voy a meterme en internet.<br><br>**JUANITA** | También tengo que hacer los deberes de español.<br><br>**GAEL** | Si tengo tiempo me gustaría pasar un rato entrenando en el gimnasio.<br>**PABLO** |

# UNIT 10 – FIND SOMEONE WHO – Student Grid

| ¿Qué vas a hacer el fin de semana que viene? | What plans do you have for next weekend? |
|---|---|
| **¿Qué planes tienes para el sábado/domingo?** | *What are you going to do on Sat/Sun?* |
| **¿Qué tienes que/ te gustaría hacer?** | *What do you have to/would you like to do?* |

| | Find someone who... | Name(s) |
|---|---|---|
| **1.** | ...would like to spend time with their family next weekend. | |
| **2.** | ...is going to play video games afterwards. | |
| **3.** | ...would like to spend an hour playing the guitar. | |
| **4.** | ...is going to do something with their friends. | |
| **5.** | ...would like to go to the shopping mall afterwards. | |
| **6.** | ...would like to play the piano on Saturday afternoon. | |
| **7.** | ...is going to listen to music on Sunday. | |
| **8.** | ...has to study or do schoolwork. | |
| **9.** | ...would like to go to the cinema next weekend. | |
| **10.** | ...is going to read a book afterwards. | |
| **11.** | ...would like to spend some time working out at the gym. | |
| **12.** | ...talks about their plans for Sunday. | |
| **13.** | ...also has to take out her dog. | |

# UNIT 10 – ORAL PING-PONG – Person A

| ENGLISH | SPANISH | ENGLISH | SPANISH |
|---|---|---|---|
| On Saturday morning, I would like to go out with my friends. | El sábado por la mañana me gustaría salir con mis amigos. | Next Sunday, I am going to listen to music. | El domingo que viene voy a escuchar música. |
| Later, I am going to play video games. | | Later, in the afternoon, I would like to do my maths homework. | |
| However, I also have to help at home. | Sin embargo, también tengo que ayudar en casa. | What do you have to do? | ¿Qué tienes que hacer? |
| What plans do you have for next weekend? | | I think it will be entertaining and fun. | |
| If I have time, I would like to spend a while chatting with my friend. | Si tengo tiempo me gustaría pasar un rato charlando con mi amiga. | However, I also have to study for a Spanish exam. | Sin embargo, también tengo que estudiar para un examen de español. |
| I think it will be relaxing. | | What would you like to do? | |
| I would like to go shopping with my friends. | Me gustaría ir de compras con mis amigos. | I would like to go shopping with my mother and play on the PlayStation. | Me gustaría ir de compras con mi madre y jugar a la Play. |
| On Sunday afternoon, I am going to look at my Insta. | | I also have to take the dog out in the afternoon. | |
| Next weekend, I would like to go fishing. | El fin de semana que viene me gustaría ir de pesca. | In the afternoon, I am going to play the piano and the guitar. | Por la tarde voy a tocar el piano y la guitarra. |
| Later, I am going to talk with friends and walk the dog. | | Next weekend, I would like to do many things. | |

# UNIT 10 – ORAL PING-PONG – Person B

| ENGLISH | SPANISH | ENGLISH | SPANISH |
|---|---|---|---|
| On Saturday morning, I would like to go out with my friends. | | Next Sunday, I am going to listen to music. | |
| Later, I am going to play video games. | Luego voy a jugar a videojuegos. | Later, in the afternoon, I would like to do my maths homework. | Luego, por la tarde me gustaría hacer los deberes de matemáticas. |
| However, I also have to help at home. | | What do you have to do? | |
| What plans do you have for next weekend? | ¿Qué planes tienes para el fin de semana que viene? | I think it will be entertaining and fun. | Pienso que será entretenido y divertido. |
| If I have time, I would like to spend a while chatting with my friend. | | However, I also have to study for a Spanish exam. | |
| I think it will be relaxing. | Pienso que será relajante. | What would you like to do? | ¿Qué te gustaría hacer? |
| I would like to go shopping with my friends. | | I would like to go shopping with my mother and play on the PlayStation. | |
| On Sunday afternoon, I am going to look at my Insta. | El domingo por la tarde voy a mirar mi Instagram. | I also have to take the dog out in the afternoon. | También tengo que sacar al perro por la tarde. |
| Next weekend, I would like to go fishing. | | In the afternoon, I am going to play the piano and the guitar. | |
| Later, I am going to talk with friends and walk the dog. | Luego voy a hablar con amigos y sacar al perro. | Next weekend, I would like to do many things. | El fin de semana que viene me gustaría hacer muchas cosas. |

# No Snakes No Ladders

| | | | |
|---|---|---|---|
| **7** I think it will be fun. | **8** If I have time, I would like to play the piano. | **23** I would like to listen to music on Sunday afternoon. | **24** Later, I'm going to look at my Instagram. |
| **6** I would like to spend time with my family. | **9** What are you going to do next weekend? | **22** What plans do you have for Sunday? | **25** However, I also have to do my Spanish homework. |
| **5** What would you like to do next weekend? | **10** I would like to go for a walk. | **21** If I have time I'm going to spend a while training in the gym. | **26** If I have time, I would like to play the guitar. |
| **4** Later, in the afternoon, I'm going to play on the PlayStation. | **11** On Saturday afternoon, I'm going to go to the shopping mall. | **20** I think next weekend will be relaxing. | **27** I would like to go to the stadium next weekend. |
| **3** On Saturday morning, I'm going to go out with my friends. | **12** Later, on Sunday, I'm going to talk with my friends. | **19** I would like to spend some time chatting with my friends. | **28** On Saturday, I would like to go fishing. |
| **2** I would like to go to the cinema next weekend. | **13** However, I also have to study for a maths exam. | **18** What do you have to do next weekend? | **29** Later, on Sunday, I have to help at home. |
| **1** What plans do you have for Saturday? | **14** If I have time, I would like to play video games. | **17** Then, in the afternoon, I would like to read a book. | **30** What would you like to do on Saturday afternoon? |
| **START** | **15** I would like to go shopping next weekend. | **16** On Saturday morning, I would like to go to the park. | **FINISH** |

# No Snakes No Ladders

| | 1 | 2 | 3 | 4 | 5 | 6 | 7 |
|---|---|---|---|---|---|---|---|
| **SALIDA** | ¿Qué planes tienes para el sábado? | Me gustaría ir al cine el fin de semana que viene. | El sábado por la mañana voy a salir con mis amigos. | Luego, por la tarde voy a jugar a la Play. | ¿Qué te gustaría hacer el fin de semana que viene? | Me gustaría pasar tiempo con mi familia. | Pienso que será divertido. |
| **15** Me gustaría ir de compras el fin de semana que viene. | **14** Si tengo tiempo me gustaría jugar a videojuegos. | **13** Sin embargo, también tengo que estudiar para un examen de matemáticas. | **12** Luego, el domingo voy a hablar con mis amigos. | **11** El sábado por la tarde voy a ir al centro comercial. | **10** Me gustaría ir de paseo. | **9** ¿Qué vas a hacer el fin de semana que viene? | **8** Si tengo tiempo me gustaría tocar el piano. |
| **16** El sábado por la mañana me gustaría ir al parque. | **17** Luego, por la tarde me gustaría leer un libro. | **18** ¿Qué tienes que hacer el fin de semana que viene? | **19** Me gustaría pasar un rato charlando con mis amigos. | **20** El fin de semana que viene pienso que será relajante. | **21** Si tengo tiempo voy a pasar un rato entrenando en el gimnasio. | **22** ¿Qué planes tienes para el domingo? | **23** Me gustaría escuchar música el domingo por la tarde. |
| **LLEGADA** | **30** ¿Qué te gustaría hacer el sábado por la tarde? | **29** Luego, el domingo tengo que ayudar en casa. | **28** El sábado me gustaría ir de pesca. | **27** Me gustaría ir al estadio el fin de semana que viene. | **26** Si tengo tiempo me gustaría tocar la guitarra. | **25** Sin embargo, también tengo que hacer los deberes de español. | **24** Luego voy a mirar mi Instagram. |

# UNIT 10 – STAIRCASE TRANSLATION

Next weekend, I would like to go to the park.

Next weekend, I would like to go to the park and spend time with my friends. I would also like to go to the cinema.

Next weekend, I would like to go to the park and spend time with my friends. I would also like to go to the cinema. On Saturday morning, I am going to look at my Instagram and read a book.

Next weekend, I would like to go to the park and spend time with my friends. I would also like to go to the cinema. On Saturday morning, I am going to look at my Instagram and read a book. Later, on Sunday, I am going to play on the PlayStation and play the piano.

Next weekend, I would like to go to the park and spend time with my friends. I would also like to go to the cinema. On Saturday morning, I am going to look at my Instagram and read a book. Later, on Sunday, I am going to play on the PlayStation and play the piano. However, I also have to help at home.

Next weekend, I would like to go to the park and spend time with my friends. I would also like to go to the cinema. On Saturday morning, I am going to look at my Instagram and read a book. Later, on Sunday, I am going to play on the PlayStation and play the piano. However, I also have to help at home. If I have time, I would like to spend some time working out at the gym.

Translate the last step here:

# UNIT 10 – TRAPDOOR

| El fin de semana que viene<br><br>El sábado<br><br>El domingo | me gustaría<br>tengo que<br>voy a | escuchar música<br>leer un libro<br>meterme en internet<br>ir al cine<br>ir al centro comercial<br>ir de paseo<br>ir de compras | y también | me gustaría<br><br>tengo que<br><br>voy a | hacer los deberes<br>mirar mi Instagram<br>ir de pesca<br>pasar tiempo con mi familia<br>pasar una hora charlando<br>jugar a la Play<br>sacar al perro |
|---|---|---|---|---|---|

## ROUND 1

1. Next weekend, on Saturday, I would like to go for a walk and I also have to do my homework.
2. On Sunday, I would like to read a book and I'm also going to go to the cinema.
3. On Saturday, I'm going shopping and I would also like to browse the internet.
4. Next weekend, I would like to listen to music and I also have to check my Instagram.
5. On Sunday, I have to take the dog out and I'm also going to spend time with my family.
6. On Saturday, I'm going to the shopping mall and I would also like to play video games.
7. Next weekend, I would like to go fishing and I also have to spend an hour chatting.

|  | Time 1 | Time 2 | Time 3 | Time 4 |
|---|---|---|---|---|
| **Time** |  |  |  |  |
| **Mistakes** |  |  |  |  |

## ROUND 2

1. Next weekend, I have to go shopping and also, I'm going to watch a movie.
2. On Saturday, I would like to go for a walk and I also have to do my homework.
3. On Sunday, I'm going to the shopping mall and I would also like to listen to music.
4. Next weekend, I would like to spend time with my family and I also have to study for a test.
5. On Saturday, I'm going to read a book and I would also like to play on PlayStation.
6. On Sunday, I have to take the dog out and I'm also going to spend an hour chatting.
7. Next weekend, I have to study for an exam and I would also like to go fishing.

|  | Time 1 | Time 2 | Time 3 | Time 4 |
|---|---|---|---|---|
| **Time** |  |  |  |  |
| **Mistakes** |  |  |  |  |

# UNIT 10 – COMMUNICATIVE DRILLS

| 1 | 2 | 3 |
|---|---|---|
| **What are you going to do next weekend?**<br><br>- Next weekend, I'd like to go for a walk. And you?<br><br>**On Saturday afternoon, I'm going to go out with my friends.**<br><br>- I think it will be fun.<br><br>**Me too!** | **What plans do you have for Sunday?**<br><br>- On Sunday, I would like to do many things, but I have to do my science homework. What would you like to do?<br><br>**If I have time, I would like to spend some time training in the gym.**<br><br>- How cool! | **Next Saturday, I'd like to play the piano. What do you have to do?**<br><br>- On Saturday morning ,I have to help at home.<br><br>**And in the afternoon?**<br><br>- In the afternoon, I also have to study for a Spanish exam. |

| 4 | 5 | 6 |
|---|---|---|
| **What are you going to do next Sunday?**<br><br>- Next Sunday, I'd like to read a book. I think it will be relaxing.<br><br>**What would you like to do on Saturday?**<br><br>- On Saturday, I would like to meet my friends. | **What do you have to do on Saturday?**<br><br>- On Saturday, I have to take the dog out and look for information for my homework. And you?<br><br>**On Saturday, I have to do a lot of things.**<br><br>- What things?<br><br>**I have to help at home but I'm also going to go shopping.** | **What are you going to do next weekend?**<br><br>- On Saturday morning, I would like to listen to music. However, I would also like to go fishing.<br><br>**Are you going to go fishing with your friends?**<br><br>- No, I'm going to go fishing with my family. |

| 7 | 8 | 9 |
|---|---|---|
| **What would you like to do on Saturday?**<br><br>- On Saturday morning, I would like to go out with my friends. However, I also have to help at home.<br><br>**Me too. I have to help at home and do my science homework.**<br><br>- I don't think it will be fun. | **On Saturday, I would like to go to the shopping mall and also go shopping.**<br><br>- What plans do you have for Sunday?<br><br>**I don't have plans.**<br><br>- Would you like to go fishing?<br><br>**Yes, I think it will be entertaining and relaxing.** | **On Sunday morning, I'm going to read a book.**<br><br>- Will it be relaxing?<br><br>**Yes, I think it will be very relaxing. Later in the afternoon I would like to play the piano. And you?**<br><br>- On Sunday afternoon, I would like to spend a while training in the gym. |

# UNIT 10 – COMMUNICATIVE DRILLS
## REFEREE CARD

| 1 | 2 | 3 |
|---|---|---|
| ¿Qué vas a hacer el fin de semana que viene?<br><br>- El fin de semana que viene me gustaría ir de paseo. ¿Y tú?<br><br>**El sábado por la tarde voy a salir con mis amigos.**<br><br>- Pienso que será divertido.<br><br>**¡Yo también!** | ¿Qué planes tienes para el domingo?<br><br>- El domingo me gustaría hacer muchas cosas, pero tengo que hacer los deberes de ciencias. ¿Qué te gustaría hacer?<br><br>**Si tengo tiempo me gustaría pasar un rato entrenando en el gimnasio.**<br><br>- ¡Qué guay! | El sábado que viene me gustaría tocar el piano. ¿Qué tienes que hacer?<br><br>- El sábado por la mañana tengo que ayudar en casa.<br><br>**¿Y por la tarde?**<br><br>- Por la tarde, también tengo que estudiar para un examen de español. |

| 4 | 5 | 6 |
|---|---|---|
| ¿Qué vas a hacer el domingo que viene?<br><br>- El domingo que viene me gustaría leer un libro. Pienso que será relajante.<br><br>**¿Qué te gustaría hacer el sábado?**<br><br>- El sábado me gustaría quedar con mis amigos. | ¿Qué tienes que hacer el sábado?<br><br>- El sábado tengo que sacar al perro y buscar información para mis deberes. ¿Y tú?<br><br>**El sábado tengo que hacer muchas cosas.**<br><br>- ¿Qué cosas?<br><br>**Tengo que ayudar en casa pero también voy a ir de compras.** | ¿Qué vas a hacer el fin de semana que viene?<br><br>- El sábado por la mañana me gustaría escuchar música. Sin embargo, también me gustaría ir de pesca.<br><br>**¿Vas a ir de pesca con tus amigos?**<br><br>- No, voy a ir de pesca con mi familia. |

| 7 | 8 | 9 |
|---|---|---|
| ¿Qué te gustaría hacer el sábado?<br><br>- El sábado por la mañana me gustaría salir con mis amigos. Sin embargo, también tengo que ayudar en casa.<br><br>**Yo también. Tengo que ayudar en casa y hacer los deberes de ciencias.**<br><br>- Pienso que no será divertido. | **El sábado me gustaría ir al centro comercial y también ir de compras.**<br><br>- ¿Qué planes tienes para el domingo?<br><br>**No tengo planes.**<br><br>- ¿Te gustaría ir de pesca?<br><br>**Sí, pienso que será entretenido y relajante.** | El domingo por la mañana voy a leer un libro.<br><br>- ¿Será relajante?<br><br>**Sí, pienso que será muy relajante. Luego, por la tarde me gustaría tocar el piano. ¿Y tú?**<br><br>- El domingo por la tarde me gustaría pasar un rato entrenando en el gimnasio. |

# UNIT 10 – SURVEY

| | ¿Cómo te llamas?<br>*What is your name?* | ¿Qué vas a hacer el fin de semana que viene?<br>*What are you going to do next weekend?* | ¿Qué planes tienes para el sábado?<br>*What plans do you have for Saturday?* | ¿Qué planes tienes para el domingo?<br>*What plans do you have for Sunday?* | ¿Qué te gustaría hacer?<br>*What would you like to do?* | ¿Qué tienes que hacer?<br>*What do you have to do?* |
|---|---|---|---|---|---|---|
| *e.g.* | *Me llamo Juan.* | *El fin de semana que viene me gustaría ir de paseo.* | *El sábado por la mañana me gustaría jugar a la Play.* | *El domingo voy a mirar mi Instagram.* | *Si tengo tiempo me gustaría pasar una hora tocando la guitarra.* | *Tengo que hacer los deberes de matemáticas.* |
| 1. | | | | | | |
| 2. | | | | | | |
| 3. | | | | | | |
| 4. | | | | | | |
| 5. | | | | | | |
| 6. | | | | | | |
| 7. | | | | | | |

# UNIT 10 – ANSWERS

## FIND SOMEONE WHO

| Find someone who... | | Name(s) |
|---|---|---|
| **1.** | ...would like to spend time with their family next weekend. | **Daniela** |
| **2.** | ...is going to play video games afterwards. | **Pepita** |
| **3.** | ...would like to spend an hour playing the guitar. | **William** |
| **4.** | ...is going to do something with their friends. | **Carlos/Víctor** |
| **5.** | ...would like to go to the shopping mall afterwards. | **Gabriela** |
| **6.** | ...would like to play the piano on Saturday afternoon. | **David** |
| **7.** | ...is going to listen to music on Sunday. | **Esther** |
| **8.** | ...has to study or do school work. | **Gael/Andrés** |
| **9.** | ...would like to go to the cinema next weekend. | **Olivia** |
| **10.** | ...is going to read a book afterwards. | **Pepe** |
| **11.** | ...would like to spend some time working out at the gym. | **Pablo** |
| **12.** | ...talks about their plans for Sunday. | **Sergio/Juanita** |
| **13.** | ...also has to take out her dog. | **Carmen** |

## STAIRCASE TRANSLATION

El fin de semana que viene me gustaría ir al parque y pasar tiempo con mis amigos. También me gustaría ir al cine. El sábado por la mañana voy a mirar mi Instagram y leer un libro. Luego, el domingo voy a jugar a la Play y tocar el piano. Sin embargo, también tengo que ayudar en casa. Si tengo tiempo, me gustaría pasar un rato entrenando en el gimnasio.

## TRAPDOOR

### ROUND 1:

1. El fin de semana que viene, el sábado me gustaría dar un paseo y también tengo que hacer mis deberes.
2. El domingo me gustaría leer un libro y también voy a ir al cine.
3. El sábado voy a ir de compras y también me gustaría navegar por internet.
4. El fin de semana que viene me gustaría escuchar música y también tengo que revisar mi Instagram.
5. El domingo tengo que sacar al perro y también voy a pasar tiempo con mi familia.
6. El sábado voy a ir al centro comercial y también me gustaría jugar a videojuegos.
7. El fin de semana que viene me gustaría ir de pesca y también tengo que pasar una hora charlando.

### ROUND 2:

1. El fin de semana que viene tengo que ir de compras y también voy a ver una película.
2. El sábado me gustaría dar un paseo y también tengo que hacer mis deberes.
3. El domingo voy a ir al centro comercial y también me gustaría escuchar música.
4. El fin de semana que viene me gustaría pasar tiempo con mi familia y también tengo que estudiar para un examen.
5. El sábado voy a leer un libro y también me gustaría jugar en la Play.
6. El domingo tengo que sacar al perro y también voy a pasar una hora charlando.
7. El fin de semana que viene tengo que estudiar para un examen y también me gustaría ir de pesca.

| ¿Qué trabajo hace tu padre/madre? | What job does your dad/mum do? |
| --- | --- |
| ¿Le gusta su trabajo? | Does he/she like his/her job? |
| ¿Dónde trabaja? | Where does he/she work? |

| | | | | | |
| --- | --- | --- | --- | --- | --- |
| **Mi padre** *My father* | | **actor** | *actor* | **hombre de negocios** | *business man* |
| | | **abogado** | *lawyer* | **ingeniero** | *engineer* |
| | | **amo de casa** | *house-husband* | **jardinero** | *gardener* |
| **Mi hermano** *My brother* | | **cocinero** | *chef* | **mecánico** | *mechanic* |
| | | **contable** | *accountant* | **médico** | *doctor* |
| | **es** *is* | **enfermero** | *nurse* | **obrero** | *labourer* |
| **Mi tío** *My uncle* | | **escritor** | *writer* | **peluquero** | *hairdresser* |
| | | **granjero** | *farmer* | **profesor** | *teacher* |
| **Mi madre** *My mother* | **trabaja como** *works as a* | **actriz** | | **ingeniera** | |
| | | **abogada** | | **jardinera** | |
| | | **ama de casa** | | **mecánica** | |
| **Mi hermana** *My sister* | | **cocinera** | | **médica** | |
| | | **contable** | | **mujer de negocios** | |
| | | **enfermera** | | **obrera** | |
| **Mi tía** *My aunt* | | **escritora** | | **peluquera** | |
| | | **granjera** | | **profesora** | |

| | | | |
| --- | --- | --- | --- |
| **Le encanta** *He/she loves it* | | | **aburrido** *boring* |
| **Le gusta** *He/she likes it* | | | **activo** *active* |
| **No le gusta** *He/she doesn't like it* | | | **apasionante** *exciting* |
| | | | **difícil** *difficult* |
| | **porque es** *because it is* | | **divertido** *fun* |
| **Dice que le gusta** *He/she says he/she likes it* | | | **estimulante** *stimulating* |
| | | | **estresante** *stressful* |
| | | | **fácil** *easy* |
| **Dice que NO le gusta** *He/she says he/she doesn't like it* | | | **gratificante** *rewarding* |
| | | | **interesante** *interesting* |

| | | | | |
| --- | --- | --- | --- | --- |
| | **un colegio** | *a school* | **casa** | *(at) home* |
| | **un garaje** | *a garage* | **el campo** | *the countryside* |
| **Trabaja en** *He/she works in* | **un hotel** | *a hotel* | **la ciudad** | *the city* |
| | **un restaurante** | *a restaurant* | **una empresa** | *a company* |
| | **un taller** | *a workshop* | **una granja** | *a farm* |
| | **un teatro** | *a theatre* | **una oficina** | *an office* |

# UNIT 11 – FIND SOMEONE WHO – Student Cards

| | | | |
|---|---|---|---|
| Mi padre es escritor. Trabaja en casa.<br><br>**ELSIE** | Mi tío trabaja como médico. Trabaja en la ciudad.<br><br>**PACO** | Mi hermana es cocinera. Trabaja en un restaurante.<br><br>**OLIVER** | Mi tía trabaja como abogada. Trabaja en la oficina.<br><br>**MIKE** |
| Mi hermano trabaja como actor. Trabaja en el teatro.<br><br>**ANTONIO** | Mi madre es mujer de negocios. Trabaja en una empresa.<br><br>**JUDE** | Mi tía es escritora. Trabaja en un colegio.<br><br>**JORGE** | Mi tío es ingeniero. Trabaja en un taller.<br><br>**DANIELLE** |
| Mi padre es peluquero. Trabaja en un hotel.<br><br>**FRAN** | Mi madre trabaja como granjera. Trabaja en una granja.<br><br>**JUAN** | Mi hermana es profesora. Trabaja en un colegio.<br><br>**RUBY** | Mi tío es mecánico. Trabaja en un taller.<br><br>**SAMUEL** |
| Mi padre es granjero. Trabaja en el campo.<br><br>**BENITO** | Mi hermano es cocinero. Trabaja en un hotel.<br><br>**ALBA** | Mi madre trabaja como contable. Trabaja en una oficina.<br><br>**EVIE** | Mi hermana es actriz. Trabaja en una empresa.<br><br>**SILVIA** |

# UNIT 11 – FIND SOMEONE WHO – Student Grid

| ¿Qué trabajo hace tu padre/madre? | *What job does your father/mother do?* |
|---|---|
| ¿Le gusta su trabajo? | *Does he/she like his/her job?* |
| ¿Dónde trabaja? | *Where does he/she work?* |

| | **Find someone who has a family member who…** | **Name(s)** |
|---|---|---|
| 1. | …works as a doctor in the city. | |
| 2. | …is a hairdresser. | |
| 3. | …is an actress. | |
| 4. | …is a businesswoman. | |
| 5. | …is a teacher and works in a school. | |
| 6. | …is a writer. | |
| 7. | …works in a workshop. | |
| 8. | … works in a restaurant. | |
| 9. | …works in an office. | |
| 10. | …works on a farm. | |
| 11. | …works as a chef in a hotel. | |
| 12. | …is a farmer and works in the countryside. | |
| 13. | …works as an actor in the theatre. | |

# UNIT 11 – ORAL PING-PONG – Person A

| ENGLISH | SPANISH | ENGLISH | SPANISH |
|---|---|---|---|
| **My brother works as a teacher.** | Mi hermano trabaja como profesor. | **Where does she work?** | ¿Dónde trabaja? |
| **He says he likes it because it's rewarding.** | | **My uncle is a lawyer. He works in a company.** | |
| **He works in a restaurant in the city.** | Trabaja en un restaurante en la ciudad. | **He says he doesn't like it because it's boring.** | Dice que no le gusta porque es aburrido. |
| **My father is a writer. He works in a school.** | | **My mother is a housewife. She likes it because it's rewarding.** | |
| **He doesn't like it because it's stimulating.** | No le gusta porque estimulante. | **She works in the countryside. She loves it because it's active.** | Trabaja en el campo. Le encanta porque es activo. |
| **What job does your mother do?** | | **Does she like her job?** | |
| **My aunt is a mechanic. She works in a garage.** | Mi tía es mecánica. Trabaja en un garaje. | **He says he loves it because it's stimulating and easy.** | Dice que le encanta porque es estimulante y fácil. |
| **She loves it because it's stimulating.** | | **My father is a businessman and works in an office.** | |
| **My sister is an actress. She likes it because it's fun.** | Mi hermana es actriz. Le gusta porque es divertido. | **He says he doesn't like it because it's not rewarding.** | Dice que no le gusta porque no es gratificante. |
| **She works in a hotel. She doesn't like it because it's stressful.** | | **My mother works as an engineer in a workshop.** | |

# UNIT 11 – ORAL PING-PONG – Person B

| ENGLISH | SPANISH | ENGLISH | SPANISH |
|---|---|---|---|
| My brother works as a teacher. | | Where does she work? | |
| He says he likes it because it's rewarding. | Dice que le gusta porque es gratificante. | My uncle is a lawyer. He works in a company. | Mi tío es abogado. Trabaja en una empresa. |
| He works in a restaurant in the city. | | He says he doesn't like it because it's boring. | |
| My father is a writer. He works in a school. | Mi padre es escritor. Trabaja en un colegio. | My mother is a housewife. She likes it because it's rewarding. | Mi madre es ama de casa. Le gusta porque es gratificante. |
| He doesn't like it because it's stimulating. | | She works in the countryside. She loves it because it's active. | |
| What job does your mother do? | ¿Qué trabajo hace tu madre? | Does she like her job? | ¿Le gusta su trabajo? |
| My aunt is a mechanic. She works in a garage. | | He says he loves it because it's stimulating and easy. | |
| She loves it because it's stimulating. | Le encanta porque es estimulante. | My father is a businessman and works in an office. | Mi padre es hombre de negocios y trabaja en una oficina. |
| My sister is an actress. She likes it because it's fun. | | He says he doesn't like it because it's not rewarding. | |
| She works in a hotel. She doesn't like it because it's stressful. | Trabaja en un hotel. No le gusta porque es estresante. | My mother works as an engineer in a workshop. | Mi madre trabaja como ingeniera en un taller. |

# No Snakes No Ladders

**START**

**1** — My sister works as a cook.

**2** — My father is a businessman.

**3** — She likes her job because it's fun.

**4** — He says he doesn't like his job because it's boring.

**5** — My mother works at home.

**6** — What does your mother do?

**7** — He loves his job because it is active.

**8** — My aunt is a mechanic in a garage.

**9** — My brother is a writer. He works in a school.

**10** — He says he likes his job because it's rewarding.

**11** — My father is an engineer. He works in a workshop.

**12** — Where does your aunt work?

**13** — He doesn't like his job because it's not interesting.

**14** — My uncle is an accountant and works in an office.

**15** — My mother works in the city. She is a business-woman.

**16** — My aunt works in the countryside. She is a farmer.

**17** — She loves her job because it is stimulating.

**18** — My sister works as a teacher.

**19** — She works in a theatre and doesn't like it because it is stressful.

**20** — He says he loves his job because it is active and rewarding.

**21** — Does she like her job?

**22** — My brother works in a school in the countryside.

**23** — My uncle works in a hotel and loves it.

**24** — My mother is a hairdresser in a hotel.

**25** — What job does your sister do?

**26** — She says she likes her job because it's not stressful.

**27** — My father says he loves his job. He is an actor.

**28** — He works in the countryside. My brother is a farmer.

**29** — My sister says she doesn't like her job because it's boring.

**30** — What job does your uncle do?

**FINISH**

# No Snakes No Ladders

| | | | |
|---|---|---|---|
| **7** Le encanta su trabajo porque es activo. | **8** Mi tía es mecánica en un garaje. | **23** Mi tío trabaja en un hotel y le encanta. | **24** Mi madre es peluquera en un hotel. |
| **6** ¿Qué trabajo hace tu madre? | **9** Mi hermano es escritor. Trabaja en un colegio. | **22** Mi hermano trabaja en un colegio en el campo. | **25** ¿Qué trabajo hace tu hermana? |
| **5** Mi madre trabaja en casa. | **10** Dice que le gusta su trabajo porque es gratificante. | **21** ¿Le gusta su trabajo? | **26** Dice que le gusta su trabajo porque no es estresante. |
| **4** Dice que no le gusta su trabajo porque es aburrido. | **11** Mi padre es ingeniero. Trabaja en un taller. | **20** Dice que le encanta su trabajo porque es activo y gratificante. | **27** Mi padre dice que le encanta su trabajo. Es actor. |
| **3** Le gusta su trabajo porque es divertido. | **12** ¿Dónde trabaja tu tía? | **19** Trabaja en un teatro y no le gusta porque es estresante. | **28** Trabaja en el campo. Mi hermano es granjero. |
| **2** Mi padre es hombre de negocios. | **13** No le gusta su trabajo porque no es interesante. | **18** Mi hermana trabaja como profesora. | **29** Mi hermana dice que no le gusta su trabajo porque es aburrido. |
| **1** Mi hermana trabaja como cocinera. | **14** Mi tío es contable y trabaja en una oficina. | **17** Le encanta su trabajo porque es estimulante. | **30** ¿Qué trabajo hace tu tío? |
| **SALIDA** | **15** Mi madre trabaja en la ciudad. Es mujer de negocios. | **16** Mi tía trabaja en el campo. Es granjera. | **LLEGADA** |

# UNIT 11 – STAIRCASE TRANSLATION

What job does your father do?

What job does your father do? My father works as a writer and a teacher.

What job does your father do? My father works as a writer and a teacher. He works in a school in the city.

What job does your father do? My father works as a writer and a teacher. He works in a school in the city. He likes his job because it is interesting and fun.

What job does your father do? My father works as a writer and a teacher. He works in a school in the city. He likes his job because it is interesting and fun. My mother is a nurse and she works in a hospital.

What job does your father do? My father works as a writer and a teacher. He works in a school in the city. He likes his job because it is interesting and fun. My mother is a nurse and she works in a hospital. She says that she likes it because it is rewarding.

Translate the last step here :

# ⏱ UNIT 11 – FASTER! 🐦

**Say:**

1. Where does he/she work?

2. He works in a company in the city.

3. He says that he likes it because it is easy.

4. What job does your mother do?

5. My mother works as a lawyer.

6. Does she like her job?

7. She doesn't like it because it is stressful.

8. She works in an office in the countryside.

9. My aunt works as a chef in a restaurant.

10. My brother works as a mechanic. He works in a garage.

|   | Time | Mistakes | Referee's name |
|---|------|----------|----------------|
| 1 |      |          |                |
| 2 |      |          |                |
| 3 |      |          |                |
| 4 |      |          |                |

# UNIT 11 – FLUENCY CARDS

| My father works as… | | He works in… | |
|---|---|---|---|
| My mother is… | | She works in… | |
| My sister works as… | | She works in… | |
| My brother is… | | He works at… | |
| My aunt is… | | She works on… | |
| My uncle works as… | | He works in… | |

|   | Time | Mistakes |
|---|------|----------|
| 1 |      |          |
| 2 |      |          |
| 3 |      |          |
| 4 |      |          |

# UNIT 11 – COMMUNICATIVE DRILLS

| 1 | 2 | 3 |
|---|---|---|
| **What job does your mother do?**<br><br>- My mother works as a cook.<br><br>**Where does she work?**<br><br>- She works in a restaurant in a hotel. | **What work does your father do?**<br><br>- My father is a teacher and works in a school.<br><br>**In the city?**<br><br>- No, he works in the countryside. | **My brother is a writer.**<br><br>- Where does he work?<br><br>**He works at home.**<br><br>- Does he like his job?<br><br>**He says he doesn't like his job because it's difficult and boring.** |
| **4** | **5** | **6** |
| **Where does your sister work?**<br><br>- My sister works in a company in the city.<br><br>**What job does she do?**<br><br>- She works as a lawyer. She says it's stressful. | **What work does your uncle do?**<br><br>- My uncle is a farmer. He works on a farm in the countryside.<br><br>**Does he like his job?**<br><br>- Yes, he says he likes it because it's active. | **My aunt works in a hotel.**<br><br>- What work does your aunt do?<br><br>**She is a hairdresser. She says she loves it because it's stimulating. And your aunt?**<br><br>- My aunt is a housewife. |
| **7** | **8** | **9** |
| **Where does your brother work?**<br><br>- My brother works in a theatre.<br><br>**What job does he do?**<br><br>- He works as an actor.<br><br>**Does he like his job?**<br><br>- Yes, he loves it because it is interesting and active. | **My father says he doesn't like his job.**<br><br>-Why?<br><br>**He says he doesn't like it because it's boring and easy.**<br><br>- My father says he likes his job because it's fun. He is a doctor. | **Where does your uncle work?**<br><br>- My uncle works in a workshop. He works as an engineer.<br><br>**Does he like his job?**<br><br>- No, he doesn't like it because he says it's difficult and stressful. |

# UNIT 11 – COMMUNICATIVE DRILLS
## REFEREE CARD



| 1 | 2 | 3 |
|---|---|---|
| **¿Qué trabajo hace tu madre?**<br><br>- Mi madre trabaja como cocinera.<br><br>**¿Dónde trabaja?**<br><br>- Trabaja en un restaurante en un hotel. | **¿Qué trabajo hace tu padre?**<br><br>- Mi padre es profesor y trabaja en un colegio.<br><br>**¿En la ciudad?**<br><br>- No, trabaja en el campo. | **Mi hermano es escritor.**<br><br>- ¿Dónde trabaja?<br><br>**Trabaja en casa.**<br><br>- ¿Le gusta su trabajo?<br><br>**Dice que no le gusta su trabajo porque es difícil y aburrido.** |

| 4 | 5 | 6 |
|---|---|---|
| **¿Dónde trabaja tu hermana?**<br><br>- Mi hermana trabaja en una empresa en la ciudad.<br><br>**¿Qué trabajo hace?**<br><br>- Trabaja como abogada. Dice que es estresante. | **¿Qué trabajo hace tu tío?**<br><br>- Mi tío es granjero. Trabaja en una granja en el campo.<br><br>**¿Le gusta su trabajo?**<br><br>- Sí, dice que le gusta porque es activo. | **Mi tía trabaja en un hotel.**<br><br>- ¿Qué trabajo hace tu tía?<br><br>**Es peluquera. Dice que le encanta porque es estimulante. ¿Y tú tía?**<br><br>- Mi tía es ama de casa. |

| 7 | 8 | 9 |
|---|---|---|
| **¿Dónde trabaja tu hermano?**<br><br>- Mi hermano trabaja en un teatro.<br><br>**¿Qué trabajo hace?**<br><br>- Trabaja como actor.<br><br>**¿Le gusta su trabajo?**<br><br>- Sí, le encanta porque es interesante y activo. | **Mi padre dice que no le gusta su trabajo.**<br><br>- ¿Por qué?<br><br>**Dice que no le gusta porque es aburrido y fácil.**<br><br>- Mi padre dice que le gusta su trabajo porque es divertido. Es médico. | **¿Dónde trabaja tu tío?**<br><br>- Mi tío trabaja en un taller. Trabaja como ingeniero.<br><br>**¿Le gusta su trabajo?**<br><br>- No, no le gusta porque dice que es difícil y estresante. |

# UNIT 11 – SURVEY

| | ¿Cómo te llamas?<br>*What is your name?* | ¿Qué trabajo hace tu madre/padre?<br>*What job does your mother/father do?* | ¿Dónde trabaja?<br>*Where does he/she work?* | ¿Le gusta su trabajo?<br>*Do they like their job?* | ¿Por qué?<br>*Why?* |
|---|---|---|---|---|---|
| *e.g.* | *Me llamo Gonzalo.* | *Mi madre trabaja como profesora.* | *Trabaja en un colegio.* | *Dice que le gusta su trabajo.* | *Porque es gratificante.* |
| **1.** | | | | | |
| **2.** | | | | | |
| **3.** | | | | | |
| **4.** | | | | | |
| **5.** | | | | | |
| **6.** | | | | | |
| **7.** | | | | | |

# UNIT 11 – ANSWERS

## FIND SOMEONE WHO

| Find someone who… | | Name(s) |
|---|---|---|
| **1.** | …works as a doctor in the city. | **Paco** |
| **2.** | …is a hairdresser. | **Fran** |
| **3.** | …is an actress. | **Silvia** |
| **4.** | …is a businesswoman. | **Jude** |
| **5.** | …is a teacher and works in a school. | **Ruby** |
| **6.** | …is a writer. | **Elsie/Jorge** |
| **7.** | …works in a workshop. | **Danielle/Samuel** |
| **8.** | … works in a restaurant. | **Oliver** |
| **9.** | …works in an office. | **Mike/Evie** |
| **10.** | …works on a farm. | **Juan** |
| **11.** | …works as a chef in a hotel. | **Alba** |
| **12.** | …is a farmer and works in the countryside. | **Benito** |
| **13.** | …works as an actor in the theatre. | **Antonio** |

## STAIRCASE TRANSLATION

¿Qué trabajo hace tu padre? Mi padre trabaja como escritor y profesor. Trabaja en un colegio en la ciudad. Le gusta su trabajo porque es interesante y divertido. Mi madre es enfermera y trabaja en un hospital. Ella dice que le gusta porque es gratificante.

## FASTER!

**REFEREE SOLUTION:**

1. ¿Dónde trabaja?
2. Trabaja en una empresa en la ciudad.
3. Dice que le gusta porque es fácil.
4. ¿Qué trabajo hace tu madre?
5. Mi madre trabaja como abogada.
6. ¿Le gusta su trabajo?
7. No le gusta porque es estresante.
8. Trabaja en una oficina en el campo.
9. Mi tía trabaja como chef en un restaurante.
10. Mi hermano trabaja como mecánico. Trabaja en un taller.

## FLUENCY CARDS

1. Mi padre trabaja como mecánico. Trabaja en un garaje.
2. Mi madre es cocinera, trabaja en un restaurante.
3. Mi hermana trabaja como profesora. Trabaja en un colegio.
4. Mi hermano es escritor. Trabaja en casa.
5. Mi tía es granjera. Trabaja en una granja *(also accept:* en el campo*)*.
6. Mi tío trabaja como peluquero. Trabaja en la ciudad.

# UNIT 12.

## My dreams and aspirations:
## What I am going to do with my life

| | |
|---|---|
| ¿Qué vas a estudiar el año que viene? | *What are you going to study next year?* |
| ¿Qué te gustaría ser cuando seas mayor? | *What would you like to be when you are older?* |
| ¿Dónde te gustaría trabajar? | *Where would you like to work?* |
| Para ti, ¿qué es lo más importante en la vida? | *For you, what is the most important thing in life?* |
| ¿Qué persona famosa te inspira? ¿Por qué? | *Which famous person inspires you? Why?* |

| **En el futuro** *In the future* | **voy a estudiar** *I am going to study* | **arquitectura** *architecture* <br> **programación** *programming* <br> **derecho** *law* <br> **magisterio** *teaching* <br> **medicina** *medicine* | **en la universidad** *at university* |
|---|---|---|---|

| **Luego** *Later,* <br><br> **Cuando sea mayor** *When I am older* | **quiero ser** *I want to be (a/an)* | **abogado/a** *lawyer* <br> **actor/actriz** *actor/actress* <br> **artista** *artist* <br> **científico/a** *scientist* <br> **escritor/a** *writer* | **informático/a** *IT technician* <br> **ingeniero/a** *engineer* <br> **profesor/a** *teacher* <br> **médico/a** *doctor* <br> **YouTuber** *YouTuber* |
|---|---|---|---|

| **Me gustaría ser** | *I would like to be (a/an)* | | | **albañil** *builder* <br> **artesano/a** *tradesperson* |
|---|---|---|---|---|
| **Creo que** *I believe that* | **voy a formarme** *I am going to train* | **como** *as (a/an)* <br> **para ser** *to be (a/an)* | | **electricista** *electrician* <br> **fontanero/a** *plumber* |

| **Más tarde** *Later on,* | **me gustaría** *I would like* | **trabajar** *to work* <br> **vivir** *to live* | **en** *in* | **el campo** *the countryside* <br> **una ciudad grande** *a big city* <br> **Japón** *Japan* <br> **Nueva York** *New York* |
|---|---|---|---|---|

| **Para mí** *For me* | **lo más importante en la vida es** *the most important thing in life is* | **aprender muchas cosas** *to learn many things* <br> **ayudar a la gente** *to help people* <br> **ganar mucho dinero** *to earn a lot of money* <br> **ser famoso/a** *to be famous* <br> **ser feliz** *to be happy* |
|---|---|---|

| **Una persona famosa que** *A famous person that* | **me inspira** *inspires me* | **es** | **Lionel Messi** <br> **Taylor Swift** | **porque es** | **talentoso/a** *talented* <br> **trabajador/a** *hardworking* |
|---|---|---|---|---|---|

# UNIT 12 – FIND SOMEONE WHO – Student Cards

| | | | |
|---|---|---|---|
| En el futuro voy a estudiar derecho en la universidad.<br><br>**DAVID** | Cuando sea mayor quiero ser científica.<br><br>**HARRIET** | Me gustaría ser artesana.<br><br>**GABRIELA** | Me gustaría vivir en una ciudad grande.<br><br>**SERGIO** |
| Voy a estudiar magisterio en la universidad.<br><br>**CARLOS** | En el futuro quiero ser escritor.<br><br>**JULIÁN** | Creo que voy a formarme como fontanera.<br><br>**VICTORIA** | Cuando sea mayor quiero ser informática.<br><br>**ALBERTA** |
| En el futuro me gustaría vivir en el campo.<br><br>**PALOMA** | Luego quiero ser abogada.<br><br>**JULIA** | Cuando sea mayor quiero ser informático.<br><br>**MIGUEL** | Luego quiero ser abogado.<br><br>**PABLO** |
| Cuando sea mayor voy a estudiar medicina en la universidad.<br><br>**JOSÉ** | Me gustaría ser albañil.<br><br>**ANGELA** | Voy a estudiar magisterio en la universidad.<br><br>**CATALINA** | Más tarde me gustaría estudiar arquitectura.<br><br>**FELIPE** |

# UNIT 12 – FIND SOMEONE WHO – Student Grid

| **¿Qué vas a estudiar el año que viene?**<br>**¿Qué te gustaría ser cuando seas mayor?** | *What are you going to study next year?*<br>*What would you like to be when you are older?* |
|---|---|
| **Find someone who...** | **Name(s)** |
| 1. ...wants to live in a big city. | |
| 2. ...wants to be an IT technician. | |
| 3. ...wants to study medicine at university. | |
| 4. ...wants to study law at university. | |
| 5. ...wants to be a tradesperson. | |
| 6. ...wants to train as a plumber. | |
| 7. ...wants to be a scientist. | |
| 8. ...wants to study architecture. | |
| 9. ...wants to live in the countryside. | |
| 10. ...wants to be a lawyer. | |
| 11. ...wants to be a builder. | |
| 12. ...wants to study teaching. | |
| 13. ...wants to be a writer. | |

# UNIT 12 – ORAL PING-PONG – Person A

| ENGLISH | SPANISH | ENGLISH | SPANISH |
|---|---|---|---|
| In the future, I want to be an actress. | En el futuro quiero ser actriz. | What famous person inspires you? | ¿Qué persona famosa te inspira? |
| Later, I would like to be a writer. | | The most important thing in life is to be happy. | |
| I believe that I'm going to train as an electrician. | Creo que voy a formarme como electricista. | Later on, I would like to live in Japan. | Más tarde me gustaría vivir en Japón. |
| For me, the most important thing in life is to earn a lot of money. | | When I am older, I am going to study teaching at university. | |
| A famous person who inspires me is Lionel Messi because he is talented. | Una persona famosa que me inspira es Lionel Messi porque es talentoso. | Later, I want to be an engineer (f). | Luego quiero ser ingeniera. |
| When I am older, I want to be a doctor. | | Where would you like to work? | |
| In the future, I am going to study medicine at university. | En el futuro voy a estudiar medicina en la universidad. | I think I am going to train as a craftsman. | Creo que voy a formarme como artesano. |
| I would like to live in New York. | | Later on, I would like to study architecture. | |
| For me, the most important thing in life is to help people. | Para mí lo más importante en la vida es ayudar a la gente. | I believe that I am going to study law at university. | Creo que voy a estudiar derecho en la universidad. |
| What are you going to study next year? | | A famous person who inspires me is Taylor Swift because she is hardworking. | |

# UNIT 12 – ORAL PING-PONG – Person B

| ENGLISH | SPANISH | ENGLISH | SPANISH |
|---|---|---|---|
| In the future, I want to be an actress. | | What famous person inspires you? | |
| Later, I would like to be a writer. | Luego me gustaría ser escritor. | The most important thing in life is to be happy. | Lo más importante en la vida es ser feliz. |
| I believe that I'm going to train as an electrician. | | Later on, I would like to live in Japan. | |
| For me, the most important thing in life is to earn a lot of money. | Para mí lo más importante en la vida es ganar mucho dinero. | When I am older, I am going to study teaching at university. | Cuando sea mayor voy a estudiar magisterio en la universidad. |
| A famous person who inspires me is Lionel Messi because he is talented. | | Later, I want to be an engineer (f). | |
| When I am older, I want to be a doctor. | Cuando sea mayor quiero ser médico. | Where would you like to work? | ¿Dónde te gustaría trabajar? |
| In the future, I am going to study medicine at university. | | I think I am going to train as a craftsman. | |
| I would like to live in New York. | Me gustaría vivir en Nueva York. | Later on, I would like to study architecture. | Más tarde me gustaría estudiar arquitectura. |
| For me, the most important thing in life is to help people. | | I believe that I am going to study law at university. | |
| What are you going to study next year? | ¿Qué vas a estudiar el año que viene? | A famous person who inspires me is Taylor Swift because she is hardworking. | Una persona famosa que me inspira es Taylor Swift porque es trabajadora. |

# No Snakes No Ladders

| | | | |
|---|---|---|---|
| **7** A famous person that inspires me is Rafael Nadal because he is hardworking. | **8** What are you going to study next year? | **23** Later on, I would like to live in New York. | **24** When I'm older, I want to be an IT technician (m). |
| **6** I would like to be an electrician. | **9** When I am older, I want to be a YouTuber. | **22** The most important thing in life is to help people. | **25** I would like to live in Japan and I want to be a lawyer. |
| **5** In the future, I'm going to study programming at university. | **10** I'm going to study law at university. | **21** Someone who inspires me is my dad. | **26** In the future, I'm going to train as a writer. |
| **4** Later, I want to be an artist. | **11** For you, what is the most important thing in life? | **20** Later, I'm going to study medicine. I want to be a doctor (f). | **27** I believe that I'm going to study architecture and law. |
| **3** What would you like to be when you are older? | **12** I believe that I'm going to train as a plumber. | **19** Which famous person inspires you? Why? | **28** Where would you like to work? |
| **2** I believe that I'm going to train as a builder. | **13** Later, I want to be a scientist. | **18** When I'm older, I want to be a writer (f). | **29** Later, I would like to train as a builder. |
| **1** Later, I want to be a teacher (f). | **14** Later on, I would like to live in a big city. | **17** I believe that I'm going to study law at university. | **30** In the future, I would like to study teaching at university. |
| **START** | **15** For me, the most important thing in life is to learn many things. | **16** I want to live in the countryside and be happy. | **FINISH** |

# No Snakes No Ladders

**SALIDA**

**LLEGADA**

**1** Luego quiero ser profesora.

**2** Creo que voy a formarme como albañil.

**3** ¿Qué te gustaría ser cuando seas mayor?

**4** Luego quiero ser artista.

**5** En el futuro voy a estudiar programación en la universidad.

**6** Me gustaría ser electricista.

**7** Una persona famosa que me inspira es Rafael Nadal porque es trabajador.

**8** ¿Qué vas a estudiar el año que viene?

**9** Cuando sea mayor quiero ser YouTuber.

**10** Voy a estudiar derecho en la universidad.

**11** Para ti, ¿qué es lo más importante en la vida?

**12** Creo que voy a formarme como fontanero.

**13** Luego quiero ser científico.

**14** Más tarde me gustaría vivir en una ciudad grande.

**15** Para mí, lo más importante en la vida es aprender muchas cosas.

**16** Quiero vivir en el campo y ser feliz.

**17** Creo que voy a estudiar derecho en la universidad.

**18** Cuando sea mayor quiero ser escritora.

**19** ¿Qué persona famosa te inspira? ¿Por qué?

**20** Luego, voy a estudiar medicina. Quiero ser médica.

**21** Una persona que me inspira es mi padre.

**22** Lo más importante en la vida es ayudar a la gente.

**23** Más tarde me gustaría vivir en Nueva York.

**24** Cuando sea mayor quiero ser informático.

**25** Me gustaría vivir en Japón y quiero ser abogado.

**26** En el futuro voy a formarme como escritor.

**27** Creo que voy a estudiar arquitectura y derecho.

**28** ¿Dónde te gustaría trabajar?

**29** Luego me gustaría formarme como albañil.

**30** En el futuro me gustaría estudiar magisterio en la universidad.

# UNIT 12 – STAIRCASE TRANSLATION

In the future, I'm going to study medicine at university.

In the future, I'm going to study medicine at university. Later, I want to be a doctor.

In the future, I'm going to study medicine at university. Later, I want to be a doctor.  What would you like to be when you are older?

In the future, I'm going to study medicine at university. Later, I want to be a doctor.  What would you like to be when you are older? When I'm older I want to be an engineer.

In the future, I'm going to study medicine at university. Later, I want to be a doctor. What would you like to be when you are older? When I'm older I want to be an engineer. I believe that I'm going to train as an electrician. For me, the most important thing in life is to be happy.

In the future, I'm going to study medicine at university. Later, I want to be a doctor.  What would you like to be when you are older? When I'm older I want to be an engineer. I believe that I'm going to train as an electrician. For me, the most important thing in life is to be happy. A famous person who inspires me is Shakira because she is talented.

Translate the last step here :

# ⏱ UNIT 12 – FASTER! 🚀

**Say:**

1. What are you going to study next year?

2. In the future, I'm going to study architecture at university.

3. Later, I want to be a scientist.

4. What would you like to be when you're older?

5. When I'm older, I would like to be a YouTuber.

6. I believe that I'm going to train as an electrician.

7. For you, what is the most important thing in life?

8. For me the most important thing in life is to be famous.

9. What famous person inspires you? Why?

10. A famous person who inspires me is Jude Bellingham because he is talented.

| | Time | Mistakes | Referee's name |
|---|---|---|---|
| 1 | | | |
| 2 | | | |
| 3 | | | |
| 4 | | | |

# UNIT 12 – FAST & FURIOUS

1. En el futuro voy a estudiar _______________ en la universidad.    (law)

2. Luego quiero ser _________________.    (a teacher (f))

3. Cuando sea mayor quiero ser _________________.    (a doctor (m))

4. En el futuro me gustaría estudiar _________________.    (medicine)

5. Creo que voy a formarme como _________________.    (builder)

6. Para mí, lo más importante en la vida es _______ __________.    (be happy)

7. Me gustaría ser _________________.    (a plumber)

8. ¿Dónde te gustaría _________________?    (to work)

9. Luego me gustaría ser _________________.    (a writer (f))

10. Más tarde me gustaría vivir en ___ _____________.    (the countryside)

| | Time 1 | Time 2 | Time 3 | Time 4 |
|---|---|---|---|---|
| **Time** | | | | |
| **Mistakes** | | | | |

# UNIT 12 – COMMUNICATIVE DRILLS

| 1 | 2 | 3 |
|---|---|---|
| **What would you like to be when you are older?**<br><br>- When I am older, I want to be an engineer (m).<br><br>**What are you going to study next year?**<br><br>- I'm going to study architecture at university. | **For you, what is the most important thing in life?**<br><br>- For me, the most important thing in life is to help people. And you?<br><br>**For me, it's being famous!**<br><br>- Being famous?<br><br>**Yes, a person who inspires me is Antonio Banderas because he is hardworking.** | **What are you going to study in the future?**<br><br>- In the future, I want to study at university.<br><br>**What are you going to study?**<br><br>- I'm going to study programming. Later, I want to be an artist. |

| 4 | 5 | 6 |
|---|---|---|
| **Where would you like to work?**<br><br>- When I'm older, I want to be a lawyer (f). Later, I would like to live in a big city. And you?<br><br>**In the future, I am going to study law. I would like to be a lawyer (m).** | **A person who inspires me is my mum. She is hardworking. And you?**<br><br>- A famous person who inspires me is Sergio Ramos.<br><br>**Ah, yes! What would you like to be when you are older?**<br><br>- In the future, I want to be a teacher (m). | **Where would you like to work in the future?**<br><br>- In the future, I would like to work in a big city.<br><br>**What are you going to study next year?**<br><br>- Next year, I am not going to study. I'm going to work in New York. |

| 7 | 8 | 9 |
|---|---|---|
| **What would you like to be when you are older?**<br><br>- When I am older, I want to be famous (m). For me, the most important thing in life is to earn a lot of money. And you?<br><br>**For me, the most important thing is to help people. I would like to be a doctor (m).** | **I believe that I'm going to train as a tradesperson.**<br><br>- What are you going to study next year?<br><br>**I'm going to study at university.**<br><br>- What are you going to study?<br><br>**I want to study programming.** | **Where would you like to work next year?**<br><br>- Next year, I am not going to work. I'm going to study teaching. Later, I want to be a teacher (m).<br><br>**What is the most important thing in life?**<br><br>- For me, the most important thing is to learn many things. |

# UNIT 12 – COMMUNICATIVE DRILLS
## REFEREE CARD

| 1 | 2 | 3 |
|---|---|---|
| **¿Qué te gustaría ser cuando seas mayor?**<br><br>- Cuando sea mayor quiero ser ingeniero.<br><br>**¿Qué vas a estudiar el año que viene?**<br><br>- Voy a estudiar arquitectura en la universidad. | **Para ti, ¿qué es lo más importante en la vida?**<br><br>- Para mí, lo más importante en la vida es ayudar a la gente. ¿Y tú?<br><br>**Para mí, ¡es ser famoso!**<br><br>- ¿Ser famoso?<br><br>**Sí, una persona que me inspira es Antonio Banderas porque es trabajador.** | **¿Qué vas a estudiar en el futuro?**<br><br>- En el futuro quiero estudiar en la universidad.<br><br>**¿Qué vas a estudiar?**<br><br>- Voy a estudiar programación. Luego quiero ser artista. |
| **4** | **5** | **6** |
| **¿Dónde te gustaría trabajar?**<br><br>- Cuando sea mayor quiero ser abogada. Más tarde me gustaría vivir en una ciudad grande. ¿Y tú?<br><br>**En el futuro voy a estudiar derecho. Me gustaría ser abogado.** | **Una persona que me inspira es mi madre. Es muy trabajadora. ¿Y tú?**<br><br>- Una persona famosa que me inspira es Sergio Ramos.<br><br>**¡Ah sí! ¿Qué te gustaría ser cuando seas mayor?**<br><br>- En el futuro quiero ser profesor. | **¿Dónde te gustaría trabajar en el futuro?**<br><br>- En el futuro me gustaría trabajar en una ciudad grande.<br><br>**¿Qué vas a estudiar el año que viene?**<br><br>- El año que viene no voy a estudiar. Voy a trabajar en Nueva York. |
| **7** | **8** | **9** |
| **¿Qué te gustaría ser cuando seas mayor?**<br><br>- Cuando sea mayor quiero ser famoso. Para mí, lo más importante en la vida es ganar mucho dinero. ¿Y tú?<br><br>**Para mí, lo más importante es ayudar a la gente. Me gustaría ser médico.** | **Creo que voy a formarme como artesano.**<br><br>- ¿Qué vas a estudiar el año que viene?<br><br>**Voy a estudiar en la universidad.**<br><br>- ¿Qué vas a estudiar?<br><br>**Quiero estudiar programación.** | **¿Dónde te gustaría trabajar el año que viene?**<br><br>- El año que viene no voy a trabajar. Voy a estudiar magisterio. Luego quiero ser profesor.<br><br>**¿Qué es lo más importante en la vida?**<br><br>- Para mí, lo más importante es aprender muchas cosas. |

# UNIT 12 – SURVEY

| | ¿Cómo te llamas? *What is your name?* | ¿Qué vas a estudiar el año que viene? *What are you going to study next year?* | ¿Qué te gustaría ser cuando seas mayor? *What would you like to be when you are older?* | ¿Qué es lo más importante en la vida? *What is the most important thing in life?* | ¿Qué persona famosa te inspira? *Which famous person inspires you?* |
|---|---|---|---|---|---|
| *e.g.* | *Me llamo Ben.* | *El año que viene voy a estudiar derecho.* | *Cuando sea mayor quiero ser artista.* | *Para mí, lo más importante en la vida es ser feliz.* | *Una persona famosa que me inspira es Ed Sheeran porque es talentoso.* |
| **1.** | | | | | |
| **2.** | | | | | |
| **3.** | | | | | |
| **4.** | | | | | |
| **5.** | | | | | |
| **6.** | | | | | |
| **7.** | | | | | |

# UNIT 12 – ANSWERS

## FIND SOMEONE WHO

| Find someone who... | | Name(s) |
|---|---|---|
| **1.** | ...wants to live in a big city. | **Sergio** |
| **2.** | ...wants to be an IT technician. | **Alberta/Miguel** |
| **3.** | ...wants to study medicine at university. | **José** |
| **4.** | ...wants to study law at university. | **David** |
| **5.** | ...wants to be a tradesperson. | **Gabriela** |
| **6.** | ...wants to train as a plumber. | **Victoria** |
| **7.** | ...wants to be a scientist. | **Harriet** |
| **8.** | ...wants to study architecture. | **Felipe** |
| **9.** | ...wants to live in the countryside. | **Paloma** |
| **10.** | ...wants to be a lawyer. | **Pablo/Julia** |
| **11.** | ...wants to be a builder. | **Angela** |
| **12.** | ...wants to study teaching. | **Catalina/Carlos** |
| **13.** | ...wants to be a writer. | **Julián** |

## STAIRCASE TRANSLATION

En el futuro voy a estudiar medicina en la universidad. Luego, quiero ser médico. ¿Qué te gustaría ser cuando seas mayor? Cuando sea mayor, quiero ser ingeniero. Creo que voy a formarme como electricista. Para mí, lo más importante en la vida es ser feliz. Una persona famosa que me inspira es Shakira porque es talentosa.

## FASTER!

**REFEREE SOLUTION:**

1. ¿Qué vas a estudiar el año que viene?
2. En el futuro voy a estudiar arquitectura en la universidad.
3. Luego quiero ser científico.
4. ¿Qué te gustaría ser cuando seas mayor?
5. Cuando sea mayor me gustaría ser YouTuber.
6. Creo que voy a formarme como electricista.
7. Para ti, ¿qué es lo más importante en la vida?
8. Para mí lo más importante en la vida es ser famoso.
9. ¿Qué persona famosa te inspira? ¿Por qué?
10. Una persona famosa que me inspira es Jude Bellingham porque es talentoso.

## FAST & FURIOUS

1. En el futuro voy a estudiar **derecho** en la universidad.
2. Luego quiero ser **profesora**.
3. Cuando sea mayor quiero ser **médico**.
4. En el futuro me gustaría estudiar **medicina**.
5. Creo que voy a formarme como **albañil**.
6. Para mí lo más importante en la vida es **ser feliz**.
7. Me gustaría ser **fontanero**.
8. ¿Dónde te gustaría **trabajar**?
9. Luego me gustaría ser **escritora**.
10. Más tarde me gustaría vivir en **el campo**.

# Unit 13.
## Talking about celebrities and role models: their journey to success

| | |
|---|---|
| ¿Qué persona famosa te inspira? ¿Por qué? | *Which famous person inspires you? Why?* |
| ¿Cómo fue su camino a la fama? | *What was his/her journey to fame like?* |
| ¿Cuándo comenzó su carrera? | *When did he/she start his/her career?* |
| ¿Qué ha logrado? | *What has he/she achieved?* |

| | | | | |
|---|---|---|---|---|
| **Una persona famosa** *A famous person* | **que me inspira** | *who inspires me* | **es** | **Emma Watson** |
| **Un/una deportista** *A sportsperson* | **que me interesa** | *who interests me* | | **Lionel Messi** **Mireia Belmonte** |

| | | | |
|---|---|---|---|
| **Él/Ella** | **comenzó su carrera** *started his/her career* | **bastante tarde** **cuando tenía 15 años** **muy joven** | *quite late* *when they were 15* *very young* |

| | | | | |
|---|---|---|---|---|
| **Al principio** *At the start* **A lo largo** *Throughout* | **de su carrera** *(of) his/her career* | **tuvo que** *he/she had to* | **creer en sí mismo/a** **ser valiente** **trabajar duro** | *believe in him/herself* *be brave* *work hard* |

| | | | |
|---|---|---|---|
| **Recibió apoyo de** *He/she received support from* | **su familia** **su mánager** **sus seguidores** | *his/her family* *his/her manager* *his/her followers* | **durante los momentos difíciles** *during hard moments* |

**Su éxito se debe a su (perseverancia, etc).** *His/her success is due to his/her (perseverance, etc).*

| | | | |
|---|---|---|---|
| **Gracias a** *Thanks to* | **su** *his/her* | **ética de trabajo** **perseverancia** **trabajo duro** **valentía** **talento innato** | *his/her work ethic* *perseverance* *hard work* *bravery* *his/her innate talent* |
| **ha *logrado** *he/she has achieved* **ha podido** *he/she has been able to* | **ayudar a personas vulnerables** **convertirse en una inspiración** **ganar múltiples premios** **llevar a su equipo a la victoria** **superar desafíos** **tener mucho éxito** | | *help vulnerable people* *become an inspiration* *win multiple prizes* *lead their team to victory* *overcome challenges* *have a lot of success* |

| | | | |
|---|---|---|---|
| **Algún día** *Someday* | **me gustaría ser** *I would like to be* | **como él/ella** *like him/her* | |
| | **ojalá pueda ser** *I hope I can be* | | |

***Author's note: you can also say "ha conseguido" as a synonym of he/she has achieved** ☺

# UNIT 13 – FIND SOMEONE WHO – Student Cards

| | | | |
|---|---|---|---|
| Él comenzó su carrera muy joven.<br><br>**LIONEL MESSI** | Gracias a su valentía ha podido superar desafíos.<br><br>**CAMERON DIAZ** | Su éxito se debe a su ética de trabajo y talento innato.<br><br>**RAFAEL NADAL** | A lo largo de su carrera tuvo que trabajar duro.<br><br>**CLINT EASTWOOD** |
| Recibió apoyo de su mánager durante los momentos difíciles.<br><br>**DAVID BECKHAM** | Su éxito se debe a su ética de trabajo y talento innato.<br><br>**ANGELINA JOLIE** | Gracias a su perseverancia ha logrado ganar múltiples premios.<br><br>**JOHNNY DEPP** | Ella comenzó su carrera cuando tenía quince años.<br><br>**KATE WINSLET** |
| A lo largo de su carrera tuvo que creer en sí mismo.<br><br>**ELON MUSK** | Recibió apoyo de su familia.<br><br>**BEYONCÉ** | Ha podido llevar su equipo a la victoria.<br><br>**JUDE BELLINGHAM** | Al principio de su carrera tuvo que trabajar duro.<br><br>**BARACK OBAMA** |
| El comenzó su carrera bastante tarde.<br><br>**LIAM NEESON** | Su éxito se debe a su trabajo duro al principio de su carrera.<br><br>**ED SHEERAN** | A lo largo de su carrera tuvo que creer en sí mismo.<br><br>**CRISTIANO RONALDO** | Recibió apoyo de sus seguidores durante los momentos difíciles.<br><br>**ADELE** |

# UNIT 13 – FIND SOMEONE WHO – Student Grid

| ¿Cómo fue su camino a la fama? | *What was his/her journey to fame like?* |
|---|---|
| ¿Cuándo comenzó su carrera? | *When did he/she start his/her career?* |
| ¿Qué ha logrado? | *What has he/she achieved?* |

| | Find someone who... | Name(s) |
|---|---|---|
| 1. | ...has had to work hard at the start of their career. | |
| 2. | ...received support from their followers during difficult times. | |
| 3. | ...thanks to their perseverance has won multiple awards. | |
| 4. | ...began their career at the age of fifteen. | |
| 5. | ...has been successful due to their work ethic and innate talent. | |
| 6. | ...began their career very young. | |
| 7. | ...had to work hard throughout his career. | |
| 8. | ...thanks to their courage has been able to overcome challenges. | |
| 9. | ...received support from their family. | |
| 10. | ...has been able to lead their team to victory. | |
| 11. | ...had to believe in themself throughout their career. | |
| 12. | ...received support from their manager during difficult times. | |
| 13. | ...started their career quite late. | |

# UNIT 13 – ORAL PING-PONG – Person A

| ENGLISH | SPANISH | ENGLISH | SPANISH |
|---|---|---|---|
| **A famous person who inspires me is Shakira.** | Una persona famosa que me inspira es Shakira. | **What was their journey to fame like?** | ¿Cómo fue su camino a la fama? |
| **He began his career very young.** | | **At the beginning of their career, he had to be brave.** | |
| **Thanks to his hard work, he has achieved a lot of success.** | Gracias a su trabajo duro ha logrado tener mucho éxito. | **She received support from their manager during hard times.** | Recibió apoyo de su mánager durante los momentos difíciles. |
| **He has been able to become an inspiration.** | | **When did they start their career?** | |
| **Someday I would like to be like him.** | Algún día me gustaría ser como él. | **Throughout her career, she has achieved to overcome challenges.** | A lo largo de su carrera ha logrado superar desafíos. |
| **What famous person inspires you?** | | **Her success is due to their perseverance.** | |
| **I hope I can be like her.** | Ojalá pueda ser como ella. | **He has been able to help vulnerable people.** | Ha podido ayudar a personas vulnerables. |
| **Throughout his career, he had to believe in himself.** | | **She has achieved to become an inspiration.** | |
| **His success is due to his innate talent.** | Su éxito se debe a su talento innato. | **What has he/she achieved?** | ¿Qué ha logrado? |
| **He received support from his family during hard times.** | | **A person who interests me is Emma Watson.** | |

# UNIT 13 – ORAL PING-PONG – Person B

| ENGLISH | SPANISH | ENGLISH | SPANISH |
|---|---|---|---|
| A famous person who inspires me is Shakira. | | What was their journey to fame like? | |
| He began his career very young. | Él comenzó su carrera muy joven. | At the beginning of their career, he had to be brave. | Al principio de su carrera tuvo que ser valiente. |
| Thanks to his hard work, he has achieved a lot of success. | | She received support from their manager during hard times. | |
| He has been able to become an inspiration. | Ha podido convertirse en una inspiración. | When did they start their career? | ¿Cuándo comenzó su carrera? |
| Someday I would like to be like him. | | Throughout her career, she has achieved to overcome challenges. | |
| What famous person inspires you? | ¿Qué persona famosa te inspira? | Her success is due to their perseverance. | Su éxito se debe a su perseverancia. |
| I hope I can be like her. | | He has been able to help vulnerable people. | |
| Throughout his career, he had to believe in himself. | A lo largo de su carrera tuvo que creer en sí mismo. | She has achieved to become an inspiration. | Ha logrado convertirse en una inspiración. |
| His success is due to his innate talent. | | What has he/she achieved? | |
| He received support from his family during hard times. | Recibió apoyo de su familia durante los momentos difíciles. | A person who interests me is Emma Watson. | Una persona que me interesa es Emma Watson. |

# No Snakes No Ladders

**START**

1. Which famous person inspires you?
2. He received support from his followers.
3. At the beginning of his career, he had to be brave.
4. She started her career very young.
5. His success is due to his work ethic.
6. He has led his team to victory.
7. I hope I could be like him.
8. When did he start his career?
9. Thanks to his innate talent, he has been very successful.
10. Throughout his career, he received support from his family.
11. Someday I would like to be like her.
12. A famous person who inspires me is Taylor Swift.
13. His success is due to his hard work.
14. What has he achieved?
15. He started his career when he was fifteen.
16. Throughout his career, he has been able to win multiple awards.
17. A famous person I'm interested in is Julen Lopetegui.
18. He received support from his followers during hard moments.
19. Throughout his career, he had to overcome challenges.
20. How was his path to fame?
21. Thanks to his family, he has been able to help vulnerable people.
22. He has achieved to become an inspiration.
23. At the beginning of his career, he had to overcome challenges.
24. Someday I would like to be like him.
25. His success is due to his family and his followers.
26. Thanks to his bravery, he has achieved to lead his team to victory.
27. He received support at the beginning of his career.
28. His success is due to his hard work and his manager.
29. I hope I could be very successful.
30. He has been able to overcome challenges.

**FINISH**

# No Snakes No Ladders

**SALIDA**

**1.** ¿Qué persona famosa te inspira?

**2.** Recibió apoyo de sus seguidores.

**3.** Al principio de su carrera tuvo que ser valiente.

**4.** Ella comenzó su carrera muy joven.

**5.** Su éxito se debe a su ética de trabajo.

**6.** Ha logrado llevar su equipo a la victoria.

**7.** Ojalá pueda ser como él.

**8.** ¿Cuándo comenzó su carrera?

**9.** Gracias a su talento innato ha podido tener mucho éxito.

**10.** A lo largo de su carrera recibió apoyo de su familia.

**11.** Algún día me gustaría ser como ella.

**12.** Una persona famosa que me inspira es Taylor Swift.

**13.** Su éxito se debe a su trabajo duro.

**14.** ¿Qué ha logrado?

**15.** Él comenzó su carrera cuando tenía quince años.

**16.** A lo largo de su carrera ha podido ganar múltiples premios.

**17.** Una persona famosa que me interesa es Julen Lopetegui.

**18.** Recibió apoyo de sus seguidores durante los momentos difíciles.

**19.** A lo largo de su carrera tuvo que superar desafíos.

**20.** ¿Cómo fue su camino a la fama?

**21.** Gracias a su familia ha podido ayudar a personas vulnerables.

**22.** Ha logrado convertirse en una inspiración.

**23.** Al principio de su carrera tuvo que superar desafíos.

**24.** Algún día me gustaría ser como él.

**25.** Su éxito se debe a su familia y sus seguidores.

**26.** Gracias a su valentía ha logrado llevar a su equipo a la victoria.

**27.** Recibió apoyo al principio de su carrera.

**28.** Su éxito se debe a su trabajo duro y a su mánager.

**29.** Ojalá pueda tener mucho éxito.

**30.** Ha podido superar desafíos.

**LLEGADA**

# UNIT 13 – STAIRCASE TRANSLATION

A famous person who inspires me is Enrique Iglesias.

A famous person who inspires me is Enrique Iglesias. He started his career very young, when he was 15.

A famous person who inspires me is Enrique Iglesias. He started his career very young, when he was 15. At the start of his career, he had to work hard and believe in himself.

A famous person who inspires me is Enrique Iglesias. He started his career very young, when he was 15. At the start of his career, he had to work hard and believe in himself. He received support from his family and his followers.

A famous person who inspires me is Enrique Iglesias. He started his career very young, when he was 15. At the start of his career, he had to work hard and believe in himself. He received support from his family and his followers. Thanks to his work ethic and innate talent he has been able to have lots of success.

A famous person who inspires me is Enrique Iglesias. He started his career very young, when he was 15. At the start of his career, he had to work hard and believe in himself. He received support from his family and his followers. Thanks to his work ethic and innate talent he has been able to have lots of success. I hope I could be like him.

Translate the last step here:

# ⏱ UNIT 13 – FASTER! 💨

**Say:**

1. Which famous person inspires you?

2. A famous person who I'm interested in is Julieta Venegas.

3. Someday I would like to be like her.

4. What has she achieved?

5. Thanks to her perseverance, she has been able to win multiple prizes.

6. She received support from her family during hard times.

7. When did she start her career?

8. She started her career when she was 12 years old.

9. Throughout her career, she had to believe in herself.

10. Her success is due to her hard work and bravery.

|   | Time | Mistakes | Referee's name |
|---|------|----------|----------------|
| 1 |      |          |                |
| 2 |      |          |                |
| 3 |      |          |                |
| 4 |      |          |                |

# UNIT 13 – THINGS IN COMMON

Write your own answers to the questions then interview four friends and make a note of what things you have in common.

| ¿Qué es más importante? | Yo *(Your own answer)* | 1 | 2 | 3 | 4 |
|---|---|---|---|---|---|
| ¿Creer en sí mismo o trabajar duro? |  |  |  |  |  |
| ¿Tener mucho éxito o ayudar a personas vulnerables? |  |  |  |  |  |
| ¿Recibir apoyo de tus seguidores o tu familia? |  |  |  |  |  |
| ¿Perseverancia o valentía? |  |  |  |  |  |
| ¿Superar desafíos o ganar muchos premios? |  |  |  |  |  |

# UNIT 13 – COMMUNICATIVE DRILLS

| 1 | 2 | 3 |
|---|---|---|
| **Which famous person inspires you?**<br><br>- A famous person who inspires me is Fernando Alonso.<br><br>**Why?**<br><br>- Because he has achieved to win multiple awards and have a lot of success. | **One person who inspires me is my mum. And you?**<br><br>- My dad inspires me. Which famous person are you interested in?<br><br>**I'm interested in Carlos Alcaraz because he's brave.**<br><br>- Yes, he has been able to become an inspiration. | **What has Lionel Messi achieved?**<br><br>- He has achieved to lead his team to victory.<br><br>**How was his path to fame?**<br><br>- At the start of his career, he had to believe in himself. |
| 4 | 5 | 6 |
| **I hope I can be like Lamine Yamal.**<br><br>- When did he start his career?<br><br>**He started his career very young, when he was fifteen.**<br><br>- What has he achieved?<br><br>**Thanks to his innate talent, he has achieved to win multiple awards.** | **David Bisbal inspires me because he has been able to have a lot of success. And you? Who inspires you?**<br><br>- I am inspired by Alejandro Sanz. His success is due to his perseverance and hard work.<br><br>**How cool!** | **Which famous person inspires you?**<br><br>- A famous person who inspires me is Cristiano Ronaldo.<br><br>**Why? What has he achieved?**<br><br>- He received support from his family during hard moments. He has been able to help vulnerable people. |
| 7 | 8 | 9 |
| **How did his career start?**<br><br>- Antonio Banderas?<br><br>**Yes.**<br><br>- At the start of his career, he had to believe in himself. He began his career very young.<br><br>**Someday I would like to be like him.** | **Did she have to work hard?**<br><br>-Yes. Throughout her career, she had to work hard and be brave.<br><br>**What has she achieved in her career?**<br><br>- She has achieved a lot. She has been able to become an inspiration. | **Thanks to her courage and hard work, Sofia Reyes has achieved a lot.**<br><br>- What has she achieved?<br><br>**She has achieved to have a lot of success and win multiple awards.**<br><br>- She received support from her followers during hard moments. |

# UNIT 13 – COMMUNICATIVE DRILLS
## REFEREE CARD

| 1 | 2 | 3 |
|---|---|---|
| **¿Qué persona famosa te inspira?**<br><br>- Una persona famosa que me inspira es Fernando Alonso.<br><br>**¿Por qué?**<br><br>- Porque ha logrado ganar múltiples premios y tener mucho éxito. | **Una persona que me inspira es mi madre. ¿Y tú?**<br><br>- Me inspira mi padre. ¿Qué persona famosa te interesa?<br><br>**Me interesa Carlos Alcaraz porque es valiente.**<br><br>- Sí, ha podido convertirse en una inspiración. | **¿Qué ha logrado Lionel Messi?**<br><br>- Ha logrado llevar su equipo a la victoria.<br><br>**¿Cómo fue su camino a la fama?**<br><br>- Al principio de su carrera tuvo que creer en sí mismo. |

| 4 | 5 | 6 |
|---|---|---|
| **Ojalá pueda ser como Lamine Yamal.**<br><br>- ¿Cuándo comenzó su carrera?<br><br>**Él comenzó su carrera muy joven, cuando tenía quince años.**<br><br>- ¿Qué ha logrado?<br><br>**Gracias a su talento innato ha logrado ganar múltiples premios.** | **Me inspira David Bisbal porque ha podido tener mucho éxito. ¿Y tú? ¿Qué persona te inspira?**<br><br>- Me inspira Alejandro Sanz. Su éxito se debe a su perseverancia y trabajo duro.<br><br>**¡Qué guay!** | **¿Qué persona famosa te inspira?**<br><br>- Una persona famosa que me inspira es Cristiano Ronaldo.<br><br>**¿Por qué? ¿Qué ha logrado?**<br><br>- Recibió apoyo de su familia durante los momentos difíciles. Ha podido ayudar a personas vulnerables. |

| 7 | 8 | 9 |
|---|---|---|
| **¿Cómo comenzó su carrera?**<br><br>- ¿Antonio Banderas?<br><br>**Sí.**<br><br>- Al principio de su carrera tuvo que creer en sí mismo. Comenzó su carrera muy joven.<br><br>**Algún día me gustaría ser como él.** | **¿Tuvo que trabajar duro?**<br><br>- Sí. A lo largo de su carrera tuvo que trabajar duro y ser valiente.<br><br>**¿Qué ha logrado en su carrera?**<br><br>- Ha logrado mucho. Ha podido convertirse en una inspiración. | **Gracias a su valentía y trabajo duro, Sofía Reyes ha logrado mucho.**<br><br>- ¿Qué ha logrado?<br><br>**Ha logrado tener mucho éxito y ganar múltiples premios.**<br><br>- Recibió apoyo de sus seguidores durante los momentos difíciles. |

# UNIT 13 – SURVEY

| | ¿Cómo te llamas? *What is your name?* | ¿Qué persona famosa te inspira? *Which famous person inspires you?* | ¿Cómo fue su camino a la fama? *What was his/her journey to fame like?* | ¿Cuándo comenzó su carrera? *When did he/she start his/her career?* | ¿Qué ha logrado? *What has he/she achieved?* | ¿A qué se debe su éxito? *What is his/her success due to?* |
|---|---|---|---|---|---|---|
| **e.g.** | *Me llamo Miguel.* | *Una persona famosa que me inspira es Lionel Messi.* | *Recibió apoyo de su familia durante su carrera.* | *Él comenzó su carrera muy joven.* | *Ha logrado ganar múltiples premios.* | *Su éxito se debe a su valentía.* |
| **1.** | | | | | | |
| **2.** | | | | | | |
| **3.** | | | | | | |
| **4.** | | | | | | |
| **5.** | | | | | | |
| **6.** | | | | | | |
| **7.** | | | | | | |

# UNIT 13 – ANSWERS

## FIND SOMEONE WHO

| Find someone who... | | Name(s) |
|---|---|---|
| **1.** | ...has had to work hard at the start of their career. | **Ed Sheeran/Barack Obama** |
| **2.** | ...received support from their followers during difficult times. | **Adele** |
| **3.** | ...thanks to their perseverance has won multiple awards. | **Johnny Depp** |
| **4.** | ...began her career at the age of fifteen. | **Kate Winslet** |
| **5.** | ... has been successful due to their work ethic and innate talent. | **Rafael Nadal/Angelina Jolie** |
| **6.** | ...began his career very young. | **Lionel Messi** |
| **7.** | ...had to work hard throughout his career. | **Clint Eastwood** |
| **8.** | ...thanks to her courage has been able to overcome challenges. | **Cameron Diaz** |
| **9.** | ...received support from her family. | **Beyoncé** |
| **10.** | ...has been able to lead his team to victory. | **Jude Bellingham** |
| **11.** | ...had to believe in himself throughout his career. | **Elon Musk/Cristiano Ronaldo** |
| **12.** | ...received support from his manager during difficult times. | **David Beckham** |
| **13.** | ...started their career quite late. | **Liam Neeson** |

## STAIRCASE TRANSLATION

Una persona famosa que me inspira es Enrique Iglesias. Comenzó su carrera muy joven cuando tenía quince años. Al comienzo de su carrera tuvo que trabajar duro y creer en sí mismo. Recibió apoyo de su familia y de sus seguidores. Gracias a su ética de trabajo y su talento innato ha podido tener mucho éxito. Ojalá pueda ser como él.

## FASTER!

**REFEREE SOLUTION:**
1. ¿Qué persona famosa te inspira?
2. Una persona famosa que me interesa es Julieta Venegas.
3. Algún día me gustaría ser como ella.
4. ¿Qué ha logrado?
5. Gracias a su perseverancia ha podido ganar múltiples premios.
6. Recibió apoyo de su familia durante los momentos difíciles.
7. ¿Cuándo comenzó su carrera?
8. Comenzó su carrera cuando tenía doce años.
9. A lo largo de su carrera tuvo que creer en sí misma.
10. Su éxito se debe a su trabajo duro y valentía.

## THINGS IN COMMON

Students give their own answers to the questions and make a note of which students they have things in common with.

# Unit 14.
## My summer and back-to-school plans

| ¿Qué planes tienes para este verano? | What plans do you have for this summer? |
| --- | --- |
| ¿Cómo vas a pasar el tiempo? | How are you going to spend your time? |
| ¿Tienes ganas de volver al colegio? ¿Por qué? | Are you looking forward to going back to school? Why? |
| ¿Cómo vas a prepararte para volver al colegio? | How are you going to prepare to go back to school? |

| Este verano | voy a ir de vacaciones | con | mi familia | *my family* |
| --- | --- | --- | --- | --- |
| *This summer* | *I am going to go on holiday* | *with* | mis amigos | *my friends* |

| Normalmente vamos a | España | pero este año vamos a ir a | Alemania |
| --- | --- | --- | --- |
| *Normally we go to* | **Portugal** | *but this year we are going to go to* | **Francia** |

| Vamos a quedarnos en | un hotel barato | *a cheap hotel* |
| --- | --- | --- |
| *We are going to stay in* | un hotel de lujo | *a luxury hotel* |
| | un albergue juvenil | *a youth hostel* |

| Voy/vamos a pasar tiempo | descansando | *resting* | en la ciudad | *in the city* |
| --- | --- | --- | --- | --- |
| | haciendo senderismo | *hiking* | en el mar | *in the sea* |
| *I/We are going to spend time* | haciendo turismo | *sightseeing* | en la montaña | *in the mountains* |
| | nadando | *swimming* | en la piscina | *in the pool* |
| | sacando fotos | *taking photos* | | |

| Durante las vacaciones | voy a | *I am going* | hacer muchas cosas |
| --- | --- | --- | --- |
| *During the holidays* | vamos a | *we are going* | *to do many things* |

| Por la mañana | me gustaría | dar un paseo | *to go for a walk* |
| --- | --- | --- | --- |
| *In the morning* | *I would like* | dormir hasta tarde | *to sleep until late* |
| | | ir a la playa | *to go to the beach* |
| | | salir con mis amigos | *to go out with my friends* |

| Luego, por la tarde | voy a | pasar tiempo | charlando con los amigos | *chatting to friends* |
| --- | --- | --- | --- | --- |
| *Later, in the afternooon* | vamos a | *spend time* | jugando a videojuegos | *playing video games* |
| | | | *sacando fotos | *taking photos* |
| | | | viendo una serie en Netflix | *watching a series on Netflix* |

| Después de las vacaciones | | Antes de volver al colegio | |
| --- | --- | --- | --- |
| *After the holidays* | | *Before going back to school* | |
| Tengo que | actualizar mi calendario | *update my calendar* | |
| *I have to* | comprar material escolar | *buy school equipment* | |
| | establecer una rutina | *establish a routine* | |
| | prepararme para mis clases | *prepare for my classes* | |

| Tengo ganas de volver al colegio | para | seguir estudiando | *carry on studying* |
| --- | --- | --- | --- |
| *I am looking forward to going back to school* | *(in order) to* | ver a mis amigos | *see my friends* |
| | | volver a la rutina | *return to the routine* |

*Author's note: You can use a few different verbs to talk about 'taking' photos, such as 'sacar', 'tomar' or 'hacer'. You can use, "tomando/sacando/haciendo" fotos to say "taking" photos.

# UNIT 14 – FIND SOMEONE WHO – Student Cards

| | | | |
|---|---|---|---|
| Vamos a quedarnos en un hotel de lujo.<br><br>**IÑAKI** | Por la mañana me gustaría dormir hasta tarde.<br><br>**ROBERTO** | Luego, por la tarde voy a pasar tiempo sacando fotos.<br><br>**DAVINA** | Tengo que comprar material escolar.<br><br>**KARINA** |
| Voy a pasar tiempo nadando en el mar.<br><br>**VICENTE** | Después de las vacaciones tengo que actualizar mi calendario.<br>**CARMEN** | Normalmente vamos a Portugal, pero este año vamos a ir a Francia.<br><br>**LUISA** | Este verano voy a ir de vacaciones con mi familia.<br><br>**SVEN** |
| Tengo ganas de volver al colegio para seguir estudiando.<br><br>**LUCÍA** | Vamos a quedarnos en un hotel barato.<br><br>**ABELITO** | Por la mañana vamos a pasar tiempo viendo vídeos en Netflix.<br><br>**YEE** | Luego, por la tarde vamos a pasar tiempo jugando a videojuegos.<br><br>**ELLIE** |
| Durante las vacaciones voy a hacer muchas cosas.<br><br>**MATT** | Tengo que prepararme para mis clases y actualizar mi calendario.<br>**BORIS** | Antes de volver al colegio voy a pasar tiempo descansando.<br><br>**DARIO** | Por la tarde me gustaría ir a la playa.<br><br>**FÁTIMA** |

# UNIT 14 – FIND SOMEONE WHO – Student Grid

| | |
|---|---|
| **¿Qué planes tienes para este verano?** | *What plans do you have for this summer?* |
| **¿Cómo vas a pasar el tiempo?** | *How are you going to spend your time?* |
| **¿Tienes ganas de volver al colegio? ¿Por qué?** | *Are you looking forward to going back to school?* |
| **¿Cómo vas a prepararte para volver al colegio?** | *How are you going to prepare to go back to school?* |

| | Find someone who... | Name(s) |
|---|---|---|
| **1.** | ...usually goes to Portugal but this year is going to France. | |
| **2.** | ...is excited to go back to school to continue studying. | |
| **3.** | ...is going to spend the afternoon playing videogames. | |
| **4.** | ...talks about sleeping in or resting. | |
| **5.** | ...is going to stay in a luxury hotel. | |
| **6.** | ...needs to update their calendar after the holidays. | |
| **7.** | ...is going on vacation with their family this summer. | |
| **8.** | ...is going to spend the morning watching Netflix videos. | |
| **9.** | ...is going to spend time swimming in the sea or at the beach. | |
| **10.** | ...is going to spend the afternoon taking photos. | |
| **11.** | ...needs to buy school supplies. | |
| **12.** | ...is going to stay in a cheap hotel. | |
| **13.** | ...is going to do many things during the holidays. | |

# UNIT 14 – ORAL PING-PONG – Person A

| ENGLISH | SPANISH | ENGLISH | SPANISH |
|---|---|---|---|
| **During the holidays, I am going to do many things.** | Durante las vacaciones voy a hacer muchas cosas. | **In the morning, I would like to go out with my friends.** | Por la mañana me gustaría salir con mis amigos. |
| **In the morning, I would like to go for a walk.** | | **What plans do you have for this summer?** | |
| **How are you going to spend your time?** | ¿Cómo vas a pasar el tiempo? | **We are going to stay in a youth hostel.** | Vamos a quedarnos en un albergue juvenil. |
| **This summer, I am going on holiday with my friends.** | | **Before going back to school, I have to update my calendar.** | |
| **Later, in the afternoon, I am going to spend time chatting to friends.** | Luego, por la tarde voy a pasar tiempo charlando con los amigos. | **Are you looking forward to going back to school?** | ¿Tienes ganas de volver al colegio? |
| **After the holidays, I have to buy school equipment.** | | **I am looking forward to going back to school to return to the routine.** | |
| **I am looking forward to going back to school to see my friends.** | Tengo ganas de volver al colegio para ver a mis amigos. | **During the holidays, we are going to spend time taking photos.** | Durante las vacaciones vamos a pasar tiempo sacando fotos. |
| **I have to establish a routine.** | | **I am going to spend time hiking in the mountains.** | |
| **Normally, we go to Spain but this year we are going to go to Germany.** | Normalmente vamos a España, pero este año vamos a ir a Alemania. | **We are going to go for a walk in the city.** | Vamos a dar un paseo en la ciudad. |
| **During the holidays, we are going to do many things.** | | **After the holidays, I have to prepare for my classes.** | |

# UNIT 14 – ORAL PING-PONG – Person B

| ENGLISH | SPANISH | ENGLISH | SPANISH |
|---|---|---|---|
| During the holidays, I am going to do many things. | | In the morning, I would like to go out with my friends. | |
| In the morning, I would like to go for a walk. | Por la mañana me gustaría dar un paseo. | What plans do you have for this summer? | ¿Qué planes tienes para este verano? |
| How are you going to spend your time? | | We are going to stay in a youth hostel. | |
| This summer, I am going on holiday with my friends. | Este verano voy a ir de vacaciones con mis amigos. | Before going back to school, I have to update my calendar. | Antes de volver al colegio tengo que actualizar mi calendario. |
| Later, in the afternoon, I am going to spend time chatting to friends. | | Are you looking forward to going back to school? | |
| After the holidays, I have to buy school equipment. | Después de las vacaciones tengo que comprar material escolar. | I am looking forward to going back to school to return to the routine. | Tengo ganas de volver al colegio para volver a la rutina. |
| I am looking forward to going back to school to see my friends. | | During the holidays, we are going to spend time taking photos. | |
| I have to establish a routine. | Tengo que establecer una rutina. | I am going to spend time hiking in the mountains. | Voy a pasar tiempo haciendo senderismo en la montaña. |
| Normally, we go to Spain but this year we are going to go to Germany. | | We are going to go for a walk in the city. | |
| During the holidays, we are going to do many things. | Durante las vacaciones vamos a hacer muchas cosas. | After the holidays, I have to prepare for my classes. | Después de las vacaciones tengo que prepararme para mis clases. |

# No Snakes No Ladders

**1** What are your plans for this summer?

**2** We are going to spend time sightseeing in the city.

**3** In the morning, I would like to sleep in late.

**4** I have to update my calendar.

**5** I am excited to go back to school to see my friends.

**6** We are going to stay in a luxury hotel.

**7** Normally, we go to Portugal but this year we are going to France.

**8** Later, in the afternoon, I am going to spend time playing video games.

**9** I have to buy school equipment.

**10** I am looking forward to going back to school to get back into a routine.

**11** Are you looking forward to going back to school?

**12** I am going to spend time swimming in the sea.

**13** In the morning, I would like to go to the beach.

**14** In the afternoon, I am going to spend time watching a series on Netflix.

**15** This summer, I am going on holiday with my family.

**16** Before going back to school, I am going to establish a routine.

**17** I am looking forward to going back to school to continue studying.

**18** We are going to stay in a cheap hotel.

**19** In the afternoon, I would like to go out with my friends.

**20** How are you going to prepare to go back to school?

**21** We are going to spend time taking photos in the mountains.

**22** Later, I have to prepare for my classes.

**23** This summer, I am going to go on holiday to Spain.

**24** During the holidays, I am going to sleep until late.

**25** We are going to spend time chatting with friends.

**26** How are you going to spend the time?

**27** In the morning, I would like to continue studying.

**28** I have to buy my school equipment to continue studying.

**29** This year I am going to go on holiday with my friends.

**30** We are going to stay in a luxury hotel in the city.

**START**

**FINISH**

# No Snakes No Ladders

**SALIDA**

| | | | | |
|---|---|---|---|---|
| **1** ¿Qué planes tienes para este verano? | **2** Vamos a pasar tiempo haciendo turismo en la ciudad. | **3** Por la mañana me gustaría dormir hasta tarde. | **4** Tengo que actualizar mi calendario. | **5** Tengo ganas de volver al colegio para ver a mis amigos. |
| **6** Vamos a quedarnos en un hotel de lujo. | **7** Normalmente vamos a Portugal, pero este año vamos a Francia. | | | |
| **14** Por la tarde voy a pasar tiempo viendo una serie en Netflix. | **13** Por la mañana me gustaría ir a la playa. | **12** Voy a pasar tiempo nadando en el mar. | **11** ¿Tienes ganas de volver al colegio? | **10** Tengo ganas de volver al colegio para volver a la rutina. |
| | | | | **9** Tengo que comprar material escolar. |
| | | | | **8** Luego, por la tarde voy a pasar tiempo jugando a videojuegos. |
| **15** Este verano voy a ir de vacaciones con mi familia. | **16** Antes de volver al colegio voy a establecer una rutina. | | | |
| **17** Tengo ganas de volver al colegio para seguir estudiando. | **18** Vamos a quedarnos en un hotel barato. | **19** Por la tarde me gustaría salir con mis amigos. | **20** ¿Cómo vas a prepararte para volver al colegio? | **21** Vamos a pasar tiempo sacando fotos en la montaña. |
| | | | | **22** Luego, tengo que prepararme para mis clases. |
| | | | | **23** Este verano voy a ir de vacaciones a España. |
| **30** Vamos a quedarnos en un hotel de lujo en la ciudad. | **29** Este año voy a ir de vacaciones con mis amigos. | **28** Tengo que comprar mi material escolar para seguir estudiando. | **27** Por la mañana me gustaría seguir estudiando. | **26** ¿Cómo vas a pasar el tiempo? |
| | | | | **25** Vamos a pasar tiempo charlando con los amigos. |
| | | | | **24** Durante las vacaciones voy a dormir hasta tarde. |

**LLEGADA**

# UNIT 14 – STAIRCASE TRANSLATION

What plans do you have for this summer?

What plans do you have for this summer? This summer, I'm going to go on holiday with my family. Normally, we go to Spain.

What plans do you have for this summer? This summer, I'm going to go on holiday with my family. Normally, we go to Spain but this year we are going to go to France. We are going to stay in a luxury hotel.

What plans do you have for this summer? This summer, I'm going to go on holiday with my family. Normally, we go to Spain but this year we are going to go to France. We are going to stay in a luxury hotel. How are you going to spend your time?

What plans do you have for this summer? This summer, I'm going to go on holiday with my family. Normally, we go to Spain but this year we are going to go to France. We are going to stay in a luxury hotel. How are you going to spend your time? I'm going to spend time sightseeing in the city.

What plans do you have for this summer? This summer, I'm going to go on holiday with my family. Normally, we go to Spain but this year we are going to go to France. We are going to stay in a luxury hotel. How are you going to spend your time? I'm going to spend time sightseeing in the city. After the holidays, I have to prepare for my classes.

Translate the last step here:

# ⏱ UNIT 14 – FASTER! 🚀

## Say:

1. This summer, I'm going to go on holiday with my friends.

2. Normally, we go to Portugal but this year we are going to go to Germany.

3. We are going to stay in a youth hostel.

4. We are going to spend time hiking in the mountains.

5. During the holidays, I'm going to do lots of things.

6. In the morning, I would like to go to the beach.

7. Later, in the afternoon, we are going to spend time taking photos.

8. After the holidays, I have to update my calendar.

9. Before going back to school, I have to establish a routine.

10. I am looking forward to going back to school to see my friends.

|   | Time | Mistakes | Referee's name |
|---|---|---|---|
| 1 |   |   |   |
| 2 |   |   |   |
| 3 |   |   |   |
| 4 |   |   |   |

# UNIT 14 – THINGS IN COMMON

Write your own answers to the questions, then interview four friends and make a note of what things you have in common.

| ¿Qué prefieres? | Yo *(Your own answer)* | 1 | 2 | 3 | 4 |
|---|---|---|---|---|---|
| ¿Ir a España o Alemania? |   |   |   |   |   |
| ¿Quedarte en un hotel barato o un albergue juvenil? |   |   |   |   |   |
| ¿Pasar tiempo nadando en el mar o descansando en la playa? |   |   |   |   |   |
| ¿Dar un paseo solo/a o salir con amigos? |   |   |   |   |   |
| ¿Jugar a videojuegos o sacar fotos? |   |   |   |   |   |
| ¿Ir de vacaciones con tus amigos o tu familia? |   |   |   |   |   |

# UNIT 14 – COMMUNICATIVE DRILLS

| 1 | 2 | 3 |
|---|---|---|
| **What plans do you have for this summer?**<br><br>- This summer, I'm going on holiday with my friends.<br><br>**How are you going to spend your time?**<br><br>- We're going to spend our time sightseeing in the city. | **How are you going to spend your time in Spain?**<br><br>- During the holidays, we are going to do many things.<br><br>**What plans do you have for the morning?**<br><br>- In the morning, I would like to go for a walk. | **Are you looking forward to going back to school?**<br><br>- Yes, I'm looking forward to going back.<br><br>**Why?**<br><br>- Because I am going to establish a routine and I would like to see my friends.<br><br>**Great!** |

| 4 | 5 | 6 |
|---|---|---|
| **How are you going to prepare to go back to school?**<br><br>- After the holidays, I have to buy school equipment.<br><br>**And before going back to school?**<br><br>- Before going back to school, I have to prepare for my classes. | **This summer, I'm going on holiday to France with my family. What about you?**<br><br>- I'm going to Spain. I'm going to spend time relaxing on the beach, swimming in the sea and taking photos.<br><br>**I am looking forward to going back to Spain!** | **What plans do you have for this afternoon?**<br><br>- In the afternoon, I'm going to spend time watching series on Netflix.<br><br>**Are you looking forward to going back to school?**<br><br>- No, I am not looking forward to it. And you?<br><br>**Yes, I'm looking forward to going back to school in order to return to the routine.** |

| 7 | 8 | 9 |
|---|---|---|
| **Normally, we go to Portugal but this summer we are going to go to Germany.**<br><br>- We are going to go to Germany too!<br><br>**I am going to spend time hiking in the mountains. And you?**<br><br>- We are not going to go to the mountains. I would like to go to the beach. | **What would you like to do before going back to school?**<br><br>- Before going back to school, I would like to rest and play with my brother.<br><br>**How are you going to prepare to go back to school?**<br><br>- I have to update my calendar and buy school supplies. | **How are you going to spend your time in the morning?**<br><br>- In the morning, I would like to sleep late but in the afternoon, I am going to do a lot of things.<br><br>**Me too. I am going to sleep late and then in the afternoon I am going to go out with my friends.**<br><br>- Great! |

# UNIT 14 – COMMUNICATIVE DRILLS
# REFEREE CARD

| 1 | 2 | 3 |
|---|---|---|
| **¿Qué planes tienes para este verano?**<br><br>- Este verano voy a ir de vacaciones con mis amigos.<br><br>**¿Cómo vas a pasar el tiempo?**<br><br>- Vamos a pasar el tiempo haciendo turismo en la ciudad. | **¿Cómo vas a pasar el tiempo en España?**<br><br>- Durante las vacaciones vamos a hacer muchas cosas.<br><br>**¿Qué planes tienes para la mañana?**<br><br>- Por la mañana me gustaría dar un paseo. | **¿Tienes ganas de volver al colegio?**<br><br>- Sí. Tengo ganas de volver.<br><br>**¿Por qué?**<br><br>- Porque voy a establecer una rutina y me gustaría ver a mis amigos.<br><br>**¡Qué bien! / ¡Muy bien!** |

| 4 | 5 | 6 |
|---|---|---|
| **¿Cómo vas a prepararte para volver al colegio?**<br><br>- Después de las vacaciones tengo que comprar material escolar.<br><br>**¿Y antes de volver al colegio?**<br><br>- Antes de volver al colegio tengo que prepararme para mis clases. | **Este verano voy a ir de vacaciones a Francia con mi familia. ¿Y tú?**<br><br>- Voy a ir a España. Voy a pasar tiempo descansando en la playa, nadando en el mar y sacando fotos.<br><br>**¡Tengo ganas de volver a España!** | **¿Qué planes tienes para la tarde?**<br><br>- Por la tarde voy a pasar tiempo viendo series en Netflix.<br><br>**¿Tienes ganas de volver al colegio?**<br><br>- No, no tengo ganas. ¿Y tú?<br><br>**Sí, tengo ganas de volver al colegio para volver a la rutina.** |

| 7 | 8 | 9 |
|---|---|---|
| **Normalmente vamos a Portugal, pero este verano vamos a ir a Alemania.**<br><br>- ¡Vamos a ir a Alemania también!<br><br>**Voy a pasar tiempo haciendo senderismo en la montaña. ¿Y tú?**<br><br>- No vamos a ir a la montaña. Me gustaría ir a la playa. | **¿Qué te gustaría hacer antes de volver al colegio?**<br><br>- Antes de volver al colegio me gustaría descansar y jugar con mi hermano.<br><br>**¿Cómo vas a prepararte para volver al colegio?**<br><br>- Tengo que actualizar mi calendario y comprar material escolar. | **¿Cómo vas a pasar el tiempo por la mañana?**<br><br>- Por la mañana me gustaría dormir hasta tarde, pero por la tarde voy a hacer muchas cosas.<br><br>**Yo también. Voy a dormir hasta tarde y luego, por la tarde voy a salir con mis amigos.**<br><br>- ¡Qué bien! / ¡Muy bien! |

# UNIT 14 – SURVEY

| | ¿Cómo te llamas?<br>*What is your name?* | ¿Qué planes tienes para este verano?<br>*What plans do you have for this summer?* | ¿Adónde vas de vacaciones?<br>*Where are you going on holiday?* | ¿Cómo vas a pasar el tiempo?<br>*How are you going to spend your time?* | ¿Tienes ganas de volver al colegio?<br>*Are you looking forward to going back to school?* | ¿Cómo vas a prepararte para volver al colegio?<br>*How are you going to prepare to go back to school?* |
|---|---|---|---|---|---|---|
| **e.g.** | *Me llamo Simón.* | *Este verano voy a ir de vacaciones con mis amigos.* | *Este año vamos a ir a Portugal.* | *Vamos a pasar tiempo nadando en el mar.* | *Tengo ganas de volver al colegio para seguir estudiando.* | *Después de las vacaciones tengo que establecer una rutina.* |
| **1.** | | | | | | |
| **2.** | | | | | | |
| **3.** | | | | | | |
| **4.** | | | | | | |
| **5.** | | | | | | |
| **6.** | | | | | | |
| **7.** | | | | | | |

# UNIT 14 – ANSWERS

## FIND SOMEONE WHO

| Find someone who... | | Name(s) |
|---|---|---|
| **1.** | ...usually goes to Portugal but this year is going to France. | **Luisa** |
| **2.** | ...is excited to go back to school to continue studying. | **Lucía** |
| **3.** | ...is going to spend the afternoon playing videogames. | **Ellie** |
| **4.** | ...talks about sleeping in or resting. | **Roberto/Dario** |
| **5.** | ...is going to stay in a luxury hotel. | **Iñaki** |
| **6.** | ...needs to update their calendar after the holidays. | **Carmen/Boris** |
| **7.** | ...is going on vacation with their family this summer. | **Sven** |
| **8.** | ...is going to spend the morning watching Netflix videos. | **Yee** |
| **9.** | ...is going to spend time swimming in the sea or at the beach. | **Vicente/Fátima** |
| **10.** | ...is going to spend the afternoon taking photos. | **Davina** |
| **11.** | ...needs to buy school supplies. | **Karina** |
| **12.** | ...is going to stay in a cheap hotel. | **Abelito** |
| **13.** | ...is going to do many things during the holidays. | **Matt** |

## STAIRCASE TRANSLATION

¿Qué planes tienes para este verano? Este verano voy a ir de vacaciones con mi familia. Normalmente vamos a España, pero este año vamos a ir a Francia. Vamos a quedarnos en un hotel de lujo. ¿Cómo vas a pasar tu tiempo? Voy a pasar tiempo haciendo turismo en la ciudad. Después de las vacaciones tengo que prepararme para mis clases.

## FASTER!

**REFEREE SOLUTION:**
1. Este verano voy a ir de vacaciones con mis amigos.
2. Normalmente vamos a Portugal, pero este año vamos a ir a Alemania.
3. Vamos a quedarnos en un albergue juvenil.
4. Vamos a pasar tiempo haciendo senderismo en la montaña.
5. Durante las vacaciones voy a hacer muchas cosas.
6. Por la mañana me gustaría ir a la playa.
7. Luego, por la tarde vamos a pasar tiempo sacando fotos.
8. Después de las vacaciones tengo que actualizar mi calendario.
9. Antes de volver al colegio tengo que establecer una rutina.
10. Tengo ganas de volver al colegio para ver a mis amigos.

## THINGS IN COMMON

Students give their own answers to the questions and make a note of which students they have things in common with.

9 783911 386173